SOUND OUT!

Ready-to-Use Phonics Activities for Special Children

Rosella Bernstein

**THE CENTER FOR APPLIED
RESEARCH IN EDUCATION**
West Nyack, New York 10995

Illustrations by William A. Stanza and Power Up! Software

Typefaces for the manuscript and cursive type in the tracing
activities were provided by Zaner-Bloser, Inc., Columbus, Ohio.

10 9 8 7 6 5 4 3

Library of Congress Cataloging-in-Publication Data

Bernstein, Rosella.
　　Sound Out!　:　ready-to-use phonics activities for special children
/ Rosella Bernstein ; [illustrations by William A. Stanza and Power
Up! Software].
　　　　p.　cm.

　　ISBN 0-87628-867-0
　　1. Reading (Elementary)—United States—Phonetic method.
2. Learning disabled children—Education (Elementary)—United
States. 3. Mentally handicapped children—Education (Elementary)—
United States. 4. Education, Elementary—United States—Activity
programs.　I. Title.
LB1573.3.B47　1993　　　　　　　　　　　　　　　　93-17470
372.4′145—dc20　　　　　　　　　　　　　　　　　　　CIP

ISBN 0-87628-867-0

**The Center for Applied Research
in Education,** Professional Publishing
West Nyack, New York 10995
Simon & Schuster, A Paramount Communications Company

PRINTED IN THE UNITED STATES OF AMERICA

ABOUT THE AUTHOR

ROSELLA BERNSTEIN received her B.S. degree in chemistry from Ohio State University in Columbus. After working as a chemist for several years and raising a family, she took undergraduate and graduate courses at Kent State University and received a certificate to teach learning disabled students in the Trumbull County (Ohio) school system.

Ms. Bernstein has taught students with learning disabilities for more than thirteen years from kindergarten through fifth grade. Because she could not find material that focused on their particular needs, she created her own. The resulting material is the basis for *Sound Out!*

A WORD FROM THE AUTHOR

Sound Out! Ready-to-Use Activities for Special Children consists of sixty units designed to help the following students learn the short vowels, long vowels, irregular vowel combinations, diphthongs, and r-controlled vowel sounds in words:

- learning disabled students
- developmentally handicapped students
- some mentally handicapped students
- students with speech difficulties
- students from the regular classroom who need extra practice in letter-sound association for vowels

This book can be used either as a stand-alone program or as a supplement to any reading program already in place.

Each unit begins with a phonogram or phonograms and a list of words constructed from the phonogram. This is followed by an exercise that reinforces the recognition of these words, a trace-say-and-copy page, and then several pages of basic reading skills activities. These skills include:

letter-sound association	word construction
recognition of phonograms	sentence construction
trace-say-and-copy	diacritical marks
reading comprehension	compound words
decoding	alphabetizing
encoding	homonyms
rhyming	vocabulary building

Included in *Sound Out!* are a complete answer key, definitions of terms, and lists of vocabulary and sight words used in the book.

When phonics is used as one of the tools for decoding new words, the frustration of haphazard guessing is decidedly diminished. Successful simple first steps establish a momentum for more positive reading experiences.

Rosella Bernstein

HOW TO USE THIS RESOURCE

Sound Out! Ready-to-Use Phonics Activities for Special Children provides the next step after the sound association for the constant letters have been learned. Emphasis is placed on the importance of learning the many vowel sounds in order to decode unknown words.

Organization of the Activities

Part One of *Sound Out!* deals with the long and short vowel letters and their corresponding sounds. Part Two presents many of the irregular vowel combinations, diphthongs, and r-controlled vowels in words.

The first page of each phonics unit introduces a vowel (or vowel digraph) in combination with a consonant (or consonants). For example, *at* is known as a phonogram. From this combination a number of words are constructed: bat, cat, mat, sat. These words should be read aloud in order to establish the letter-sound relationship. Following the list (or lists of words) is an exercise designed to reinforce this skill. Three choices of similarly constructed words are given. The student selects the one word that makes sense in the sentence. This type of learning combines the mechanics of reading with reading comprehension in an effective but non-frustrating way. The vocabulary is tightly controlled. Only words from that lesson plus previously learned words and sight words are used. Pictures are sometimes substituted for words not yet learned.

On the second page of each phonics unit, the student simultaneously traces over the word and pronounces the sounds. After the tracing-saying activity, space is provided for writing the words.

The rest of the pages in each phonics unit is made up of various activities directly related to the words in that unit. Words from previous units are also included as often as possible to provide review and reinforcement. One of the activities that merits special attention contains sentences with multisyllable words. At first glance these words may seem incongruous at this reading level. The purpose, however, is to show the student that many words begin with sounds already learned. For example, in the sentence "Ted will mail the *let*ter for me," the word *letter* is not yet in the reading vocabulary of the student but the word *let* is, as are the other words in the sentence. Even when the first syllable of a word is a nonsense syllable (such as *lem* in *lemon*), knowing the sound of the first syllable in the word aids the student in decoding the entire word. Help the student recognize new words that fit this type of pattern.

Other activities include:

- reading comprehension
- decoding
- encoding
- rhyming words
- making a word from scrambled letters
- making a compound word from two separate words
- learning to use long and short diacritical marks
- learning new vocabulary words
- distinguishing the spelling and meaning in homonyms
- figure-ground discrimination

The last page of each phonics unit has a checklist of words in alphabetical order. This gives the student additional practice in word recognition and at the same time provides you with a means of evaluating the student's progress.

Additional Strategies

Here are the four R's for making the process of learning to read easier and more enjoyable for both you and your students.

1. *REVIEW:* Keep tabs of all the words that give the student difficulty. Make flash cards or a check list and check on these often. Constant reinforcement is necessary. The goal is for the student to gain instant recognition of as many words as possible.

2. *RECITE:* Give the student a poem, short story, recipe, or joke and have him or her practice reading it until the material can be read with ease. Make a window card (see the illustration) and isolate various words from the rest of the text. See if the student can recognize the words out of context as well as in context. (Will the student be able to recognize that word in another reading situation?) Then have the student read the practiced material to the class, principal, parents, etc.

window card

3. *REVISE:* Children love to be in plays. Many of the stories in their reading textbooks can easily be rewritten into a shortened play form. Be sure to include all the new vocabulary words. Give the main character to the student who needs the most practice in reading. Take any opportunity to present the play to the student's own class or to other classes.

4. *REKINDLE:* Rekindle the enthusiastic spirit of learning to read through simply devised games that can be adapted from commonly known games such as "Go Fish," "Concentration," and "Dominoes."

DEFINITIONS OF TERMS

1. **Short vowels** are *a* as in *apple*   **Long vowels** are *a* as in *acorn*
   e as in *elephant*   *e* as in *eagle*
   i as in *igloo*   *i* as in *ice*
   o as in *octopus*   *o* as in *oboe*
   u as in *umbrella*   *u* as in *unicorn*

   Sometimes *y* and *w* are considered vowels.

2. **Consonants** are all the other letters of the alphabet that are not vowels.

3. A **Digraph** is two successive letters used together to make a single sound.
   Example of a consonant digraph: sh as in ship
   Example of a vowel digraph: ea as in each

4. **Irregular Vowel Combinations** consist of a double vowel that does not follow the regular double vowel rule.
   Examples: oo as in moon   aw as in lawn

5. **Diphthongs** are two successive identifiable sounds blended together to represent a sound within the same syllable.
   Examples: oi as in oil   ou as in out

6. An **R-controlled Vowel** is a vowel sound that is altered when the letter r follows in immediate succession.
   Examples: barn   her   fir   corn   curl

7. **Phonics** is a method of reading instruction that teaches the relationship between the symbol (letter) and the speech sound.
   Reading aloud is a form of decoding. *(Symbol to Sound)*
   Spelling is a form of encoding. *(Sound to Symbol)*

8. A **Sight Word** is a word the student learns to read after having viewed it many times. The use of flash cards is a common method of teaching sight words.

   Lists of sight words often include words that are not easily decoded by phonics.
   Examples: what   who   one   said   they

9. The **Inductive Approach** puts special importance on making many observations and then drawing a general conclusion. The phonics method of instruction in this book embraces the inductive approach.

10. A **Phonogram** is a sequence of letters that have the same sound in several words.
    Examples: ake as in bake, cake, lake, make

PART ONE VOCABULARY

back	cod	fog	jump	night	rock	stick
bad	cog	fox	keep	nine	rod	still
bag	cone	frog	lace	nose	Rome	sub
bake	cot	fuel	lay	not	rope	sum
bat	crash	fume	leak	nut	rose	sun
beak	cub	fun	lean	pace	row	swam
beam	Cuba	fuse	leg	pack	rub	tack
bean	cube	future	lick	pad	rug	tag
beat	cue	game	lid	pail	run	take
bed	cupid	gave	lie	pain	sack	tame
beep	cut	gem	light	Pam	sad	tap
beet	cute	get	like	pay	sail	team
beg	Dad	glad	lime	peck	Sam	tell
bell	dash	goat	lip	peek	same	test
best	day	grow	lit	peg	sat	that
bet	deck	gum	live	pen	save	them
big	deed	gun	load	pet	say	then
bike	deep	had	loan	pick	seat	thick
bill	den	ham	lock	pie	seed	thin
bit	dice	hat	log	pig	seek	thump
black	did	hay	low	pike	sell	tick
boat	die	heat	luck	pile	shack	tie
bone	dig	hem	lump	pin	shake	tile
bow	dim	hen	lunch	pipe	shame	time
box	dime	hid	mad	pit	shave	tip
buck	dip	hide	mail	place	shed	toad
bug	dish	high	main	plan	sheep	toe
bugle	dive	hike	man	pod	sheet	tone
bum	doe	hill	map	poke	shell	tot
bump	dog	him	mash	pole	shin	train
bunch	dome	hip	mat	pop	shine	trash
but	dot	hit	may	pose	ship	trick
cake	duck	hive	mean	pot	shock	unicorn
can	dug	hoe	meat	puck	shop	unicycle
cap	dump	hole	meet	punch	shot	uniform
cash	face	home	men	pupil	show	use
cat	fail	hop	mice	race	shut	van
cave	fan	hope	mile	rag	sick	vet
chat	fat	hose	mine	rain	side	wag
cheat	fed	hot	moan	rake	sigh	wake
check	feed	hug	mob	rash	sit	wave
cheek	feet	huge	mole	rat	skin	way
chest	fell	hum	mop	ray	slam	weak
chick	fight	human	mow	red	sled	weed
chill	file	hunch	mug	rest	sleep	week
chime	fill	hut	mule	rice	slow	wet
chin	fin	itch	museum	rid	smell	wheat
chip	fine	jam	music	ride	snack	wide
chop	fish	jeep	nail	right	snow	will
clam	fit	jet	nap	rim	sob	win
clap	five	jig	neck	ripe	sock	wipe
clock	flag	job	nest	road	space	wish
coat	flake	joke	nice	rob	stem	woke

PART ONE SIGHT WORDS

all	came	green	let	or	ten	way
am	can	had	like	out	that	we
an	come	has	little	over	the	went
and	could	have	look	play	them	were
are	did	he	made	pretty	they	what
around	do	help	make	ran	this	when
as	down	her	may	red	three	where
ask	fast	here	me	run	to	white
at	five	him	my	said	today	who
away	for	his	new	saw	too	will
be	from	if	no	say	two	with
before	funny	in	not	see	under	yellow
better	gave	into	now	sit	up	you
big	get	is	of	so	us	your
black	give	it	off	some	use	
blue	go	its	old	soon	very	
but	good	know	on	stop	want	
by	got	laugh	one	take	was	

PART TWO VOCABULARY

all
ark
art
ball
bar
bark
bawl
bear
berry
blouse
blue
blur
boil
boo
book
born
bought
bound
bout
bow
boy
brawl
bread
breath
broil
brook
brought
brow
brown
bruise
bull
bur
burn
burp
call
car
carry
cart
caught
cause

chalk
chart
cherry
chew
claw
clear
clerk
clown
clue
coil
coin
coo
cook
cool
cork
corn
could
cow
crawl
crew
croup
crown
cruise
curl
dark
dart
dawn
dead
dear
death
dew
dirt
dorm
down
draw
drawn
dread
drown
due
dune

Earl
earn
eight
fall
far
fawn
fear
feather
ferry
fir
flew
flirt
flue
foil
fool
fork
form
fort
fought
found
freight
frown
fruit
full
fur
furl
germ
girl
glue
good
gown
ground
group
Harry
haul
head
health
hear
heart
hearth

hearty
her
herb
hood
hook
horn
hound
house
how
hurl
jar
jaw
jerk
Jerry
join
joint
joy
June
Kerry
knew
Larry
law
lawn
learn
leather
look
louse
mall
mark
marry
maul
merry
moo
moon
mouse
near
new
noon
now
ought

ought
out
park
part
Paul
pause
paw
pawn
pearl
per
perk
Perry
plow
point
pool
pork
port
pound
pout
pow
prune
pull
raw
read
rein
round
Roy
saw
scout
screw
shawl
shirt
shook
short
should
shout
sir
skirt
slaw
sleigh

slur
slurp
small
soil
soon
sort
sound
soup
spark
spear
spoil
spool
spoon
sport
spout
spread
squirt
stalk
stall
star
start
stew
stir
stood
stork
storm
straw
Sue
suit
talk
tar
tart
taught
tear
tear (rip)
thaw
thought
thread
threw
took

tool
torn
town
toy
tread
true
tune
turn
twirl
vein
walk
wall
war
warm
warmth
warn
warp
wart
wealth
weather
weigh
weight
whirl
wood
word
work
world
worm
worn
worth
would
wow
yawn
year
zoo

© 1993 by Rosella Bernstein

xv

PART TWO SIGHT WORDS

about	did	had	little	open	take	went
all	do	has	long	our	tall	were
an	does	have	look	out	ten	what
and	done	help	made	over	that	when
around	down	her	make	play	the	where
at	every	here	many	please	there	which
away	far	his	me	pretty	this	white
be	first	how	much	put	three	who
best	five	if	must	read	to	will
better	for	in	my	right	today	with
big	from	into	new	said	too	work
blue	funny	is	not	saw	under	would
brown	gave	it	now	say	us	yes
but	get	its	of	small	use	you
by	give	just	off	so	very	your
call	good	keep	old	some	was	
can	got	let	on	soon	we	
could	grow	like	one	start	well	

CONTENTS

PART ONE

PHONOGRAMS

PART ONE

Activities for Long and
Short Vowels

Name _____ Date _____

1. Have the pupil go over the lists of words at the top of the exercise.
   Point out to the student that the ending of each word is the same. Examples: c*at* b*at* h*at*.
2. Next have the student do the exercises, crossing out the two words that are incorrect.
3. When all the sentences have been done this way, the student goes back to the first sentence and *orally* reads each sentence with the correct word.

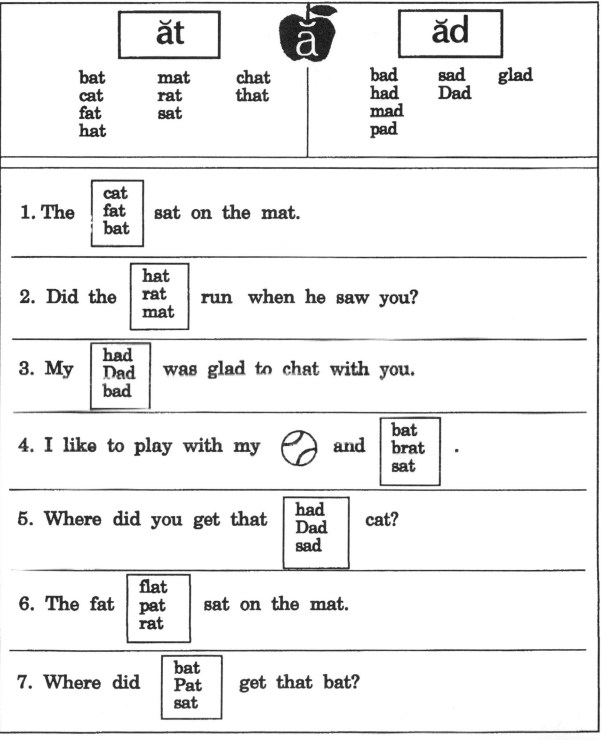

ăt		
bat	mat	chat
cat	rat	that
fat	sat	
hat		

ăd		
bad	sad	glad
had	Dad	
mad		
pad		

1. The | cat / fat / bat | sat on the mat.

2. Did the | hat / rat / mat | run when he saw you?

3. My | had / Dad / bad | was glad to chat with you.

4. I like to play with my ⊘ and | bat / brat / sat | .

5. Where did you get that | had / Dad / sad | cat?

6. The fat | flat / pat / rat | sat on the mat.

7. Where did | bat / Pat / sat | get that bat?

Name _____   Date _____

Trace over the word three or four times. Next write the words in the space provided.

This side for those who print.   This side for those who use cursive.

at   *at*

bat   *bat*

fat   *fat*

sat   *sat*

ad   *ad*

mad   *mad*

bad   *bad*

sad   *sad*

4

Name _____   Date _____

I. Write the name of the picture in the blank.
   Look for the word in the puzzle and draw a line around it.

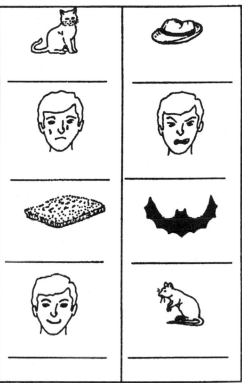

b	d	s	a	d	c	g	h	m	a	t
f	c	b	a	t	b	j	m	t	c	e
a	p	v	b	q	g	o	b	d	o	e
f	d	c	a	t	e	g	u	r	d	b
m	f	a	e	n	x	m	h	a	t	l
y	t	r	a	i	s	d	r	a	t	o
k	g	a	g	g	l	a	d	e	p	c
j	i	m	e	d	a	g	q	s	k	f
s	s	t	d	h	i	m	a	d	b	z

II. Put a line under the words that go with the picture.

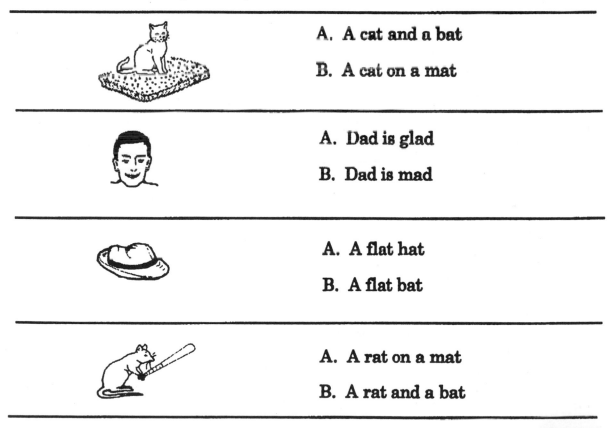

A. A cat and a bat

B. A cat on a mat

A. Dad is glad

B. Dad is mad

A. A flat hat

B. A flat bat

A. A rat on a mat

B. A rat and a bat

Name _____   Date _____

1. I want that 🍎.

   I will get a <u>lad</u>der and go up in the 🌳.   ladder

2. This ✉ is for me.

   It has my <u>add</u>ress on it.   address

3. The 👦 has a new <u>rat</u>tle.   rattle

4. This 🚗 will not go.

   We will get a <u>bat</u>tery for it.   battery

The Cat and the Rat

A rat a rat sat on a mat.

A cat a cat sat on a mat.

The rat the rat was very fat.

The cat the cat was not so fat.

The rat the rat is not on the mat.

But now the cat is very fat.

Where is that rat that fat fat rat?

Where is that rat that sat on the mat?

*The minimum number of words expected to be read per minute is 85. There are 69 words in this poem (including title). With practice the student should be able to read it in about 49 seconds.

6

Name _____   Date _____

1. Have the pupil go over the lists of words at the top of the exercise.
   Point out to the pupil that the ending of each word is the same. Examples: b*ag*   t*ag*   r*ag*.
2. Next have the student do the exercise, crossing out the two words that are incorrect.
3. When all the sentences have been done in this way, the pupil goes back to the first sentence and *orally* reads each
   sentence with the correct word.

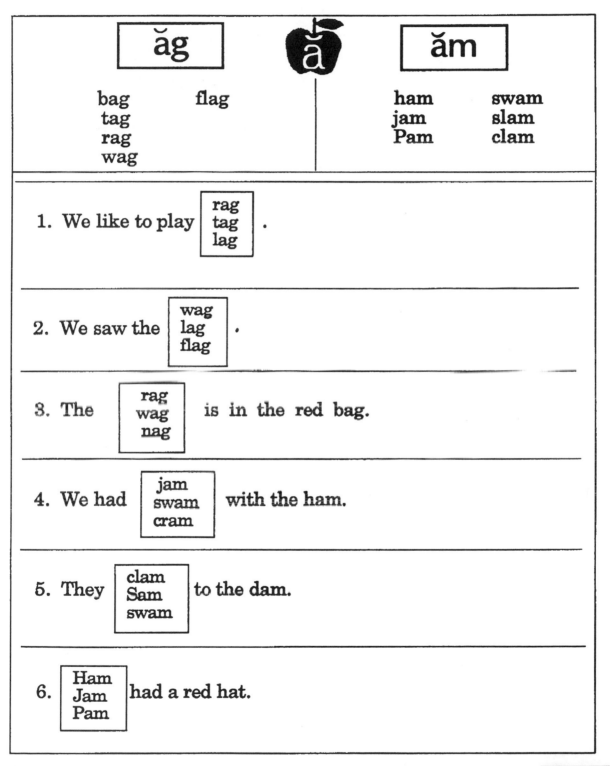

ăg

ăm

bag	flag
tag	
rag	
wag	

ham	swam
jam	slam
Pam	clam

1. We like to play | rag / tag / lag | .

2. We saw the | wag / lag / flag | .

3. The | rag / wag / nag | is in the **red bag**.

4. We had | jam / swam / cram | with the ham.

5. They | clam / Sam / swam | to the dam.

6. | Ham / Jam / Pam | had a red hat.

Trace over the word three or four times. Next, write the word in the space provided.

This side for those who print.   This side for those who use cursive.

ag   _ag_

rag   _rag_

tag   _tag_

wag   _wag_

am   _am_

Sam   _Sam_

dam   _dam_

jam   _jam_

Name _____   Date _____

I. Match the words with the pictures by writing the letter in the blank.

_____

A. A bag and a rag

_____

B. Jam and ham

_____

C. A dam and a clam

_____

D. A snag on a flag

_____

II. Write the name of the picture in the blank.
   Look for the word in the puzzle and draw a line around it.

a	o	x	q	c	a	m	b	c	z
n	c	l	a	m	v	h	a	m	w
o	u	z	r	a	g	t	r	i	j
n	a	b	a	g	g	b	w	v	y
m	t	g	f	e	l	h	t	a	g
c	d	e	j	a	m	z	g	j	v
v	o	y	p	i	f	l	a	g	x
c	w	a	g	c	s	j	l	i	o
s	g	a	n	w	m	k	d	a	m
a	v	u	s	t	z	r	m	q	z

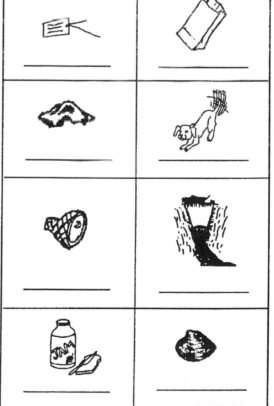

© 1993 by Rosella Bernstein

9

Name _____   Date _____

This exercise is designed to help the student figure out multisyllable words using the basic skills learned in this lesson plus context clues. The pupil is not expected to be able to read the words the first time around. Practice helps.

1. I will get 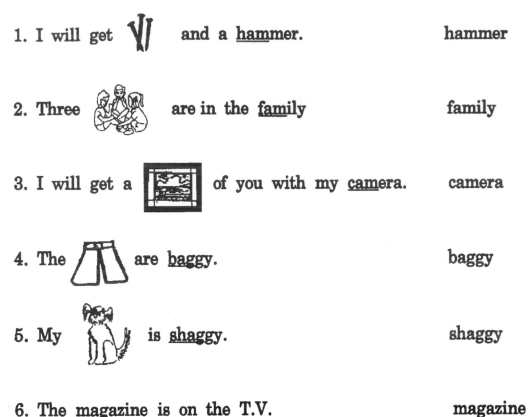 and a <u>ham</u>mer.   hammer

2. Three [image] are in the <u>fam</u>ily   family

3. I will get a [image] of you with my <u>cam</u>era.   camera

4. The [image] are <u>bag</u>gy.   baggy

5. My [image] is <u>shag</u>gy.   shaggy

6. The <u>mag</u>azine is on the T.V.   magazine

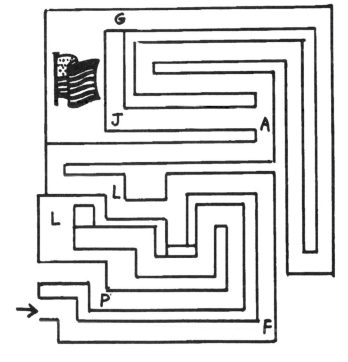

A-MAZE-ING

_ _ _ _ _

Name _____   Date _____

1. Have the pupil go over the list of words at the top of the exercise.
   Point out to the pupil that the ending of each word is the same.   Examples: *can*   *fan*   *man*.
2. Next have the student do the exercise, crossing out the two words that are incorrect.
3. When all the sentences have been done in this way, the pupil returns to the first sentence and *orally* reads each
   sentence with the correct word.

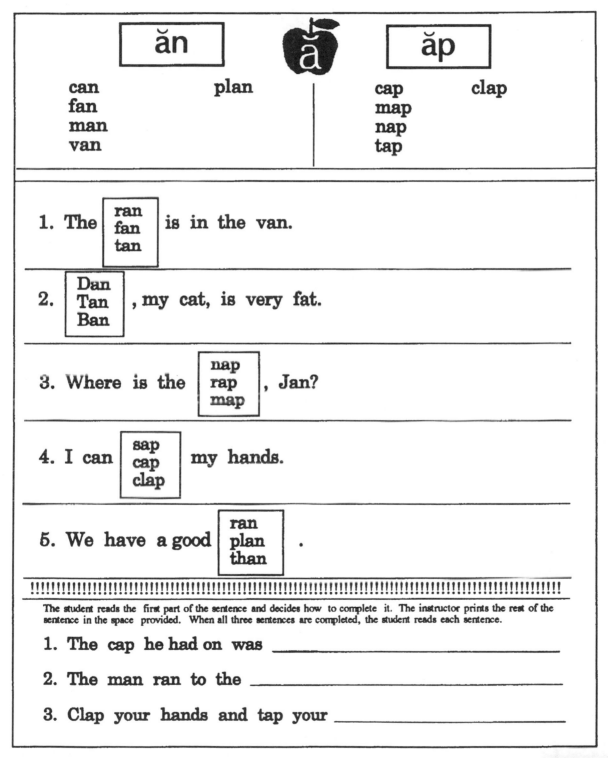

ăn		ă	ăp	
can	plan		cap	clap
fan			map	
man			nap	
van			tap	

1. The | ran / fan / tan | is in the van.

2. | Dan / Tan / Ban | , my cat, is very fat.

3. Where is the | nap / rap / map | , Jan?

4. I can | sap / cap / clap | my hands.

5. We have a good | ran / plan / than | .

!!

The student reads the first part of the sentence and decides how to complete it. The instructor prints the rest of the
sentence in the space provided. When all three sentences are completed, the student reads each sentence.

1. The cap he had on was _____

2. The man ran to the _____

3. Clap your hands and tap your _____

11

Name _____   Date _____

Trace over the word three or four times. Next, write the word in the space provided.

This side for those who print.   This side for those who use cursive.

an   *an*

fan   *fan*

van   *van*

Dan   *Dan*

ap   *ap*

lap   *lap*

rap   *rap*

sap   *sap*

Name _____   Date _____

I.

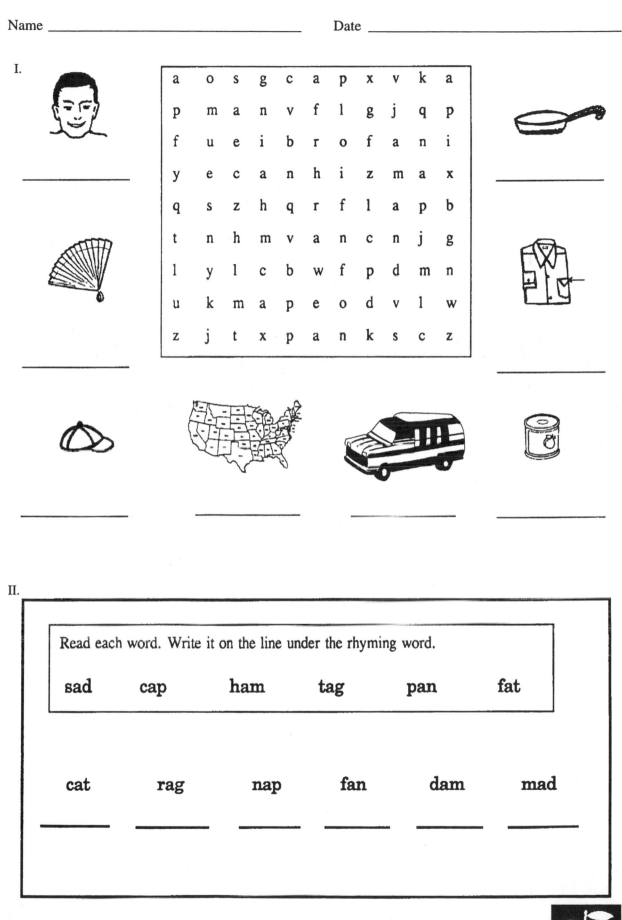

II.

Read each word. Write it on the line under the rhyming word.

sad	cap	ham	tag	pan	fat

cat	rag	nap	fan	dam	mad
___	___	___	___	___	___

Name _____   Date _____

This exercise is designed to help the student figure out multisyllable words using the basic skills learned in this lesson plus context clues. The pupil is not expected to be able to read the words the first time around. Practice helps.

1. The <u>nap</u>kins are on the ⬚ .   napkins

2. I am <u>hap</u>py that you are here.   happy

3. What is the <u>cap</u>ital of ⬚ Ohio ?   capital

4. <u>Jan</u>uary is on the ⬚ .   January

5. I like to have jam with my <u>pan</u>cakes.   pancakes

6. The ☼ is not a <u>pla</u>net.   planet

   It is a ☆ .

Find the rhyming word and put a line around it.

can	fat	fan	flap
van	man	mat	map
map	tap	tan	that
cap	can	cat	clap
nap	hat	trap	pan

Name _____   Date _____

I. Unscramble these words.

jma _____	gar _____	gba _____	amn _____
acp _____	fna _____	ahm _____	cna _____
tac _____	dba _____	tha _____	lfga _____
Pma _____	dsa _____	lpca _____	slma _____

II. Unscramble the following words.

nva   mpa   aDd   hte   dah   a   ni

_____   _____   _____   _____   _____   _____   _____

Now rearrange the words to make a sentence. Write it on the line.

_____

Name ______________________________ Date ______________________________

1. Have the pupil go over the list of words at the top of the exercise.
   Point out to the pupil that the ending of each word is the same. Examples: b*ack* s*ack* t*ack*.
2. Next have the pupil do the exercises, crossing out the two words that are incorrect.
3. When all the sentences have been done in this way, the pupil returns to the first sentence and *orally* reads each sentence with the correct word.

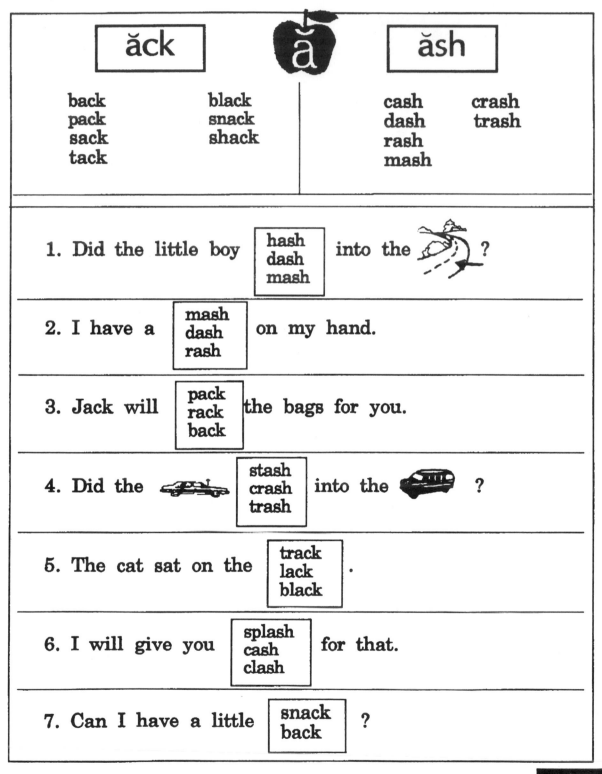

ăck		ăsh	
back	black	cash	crash
pack	snack	dash	trash
sack	shack	rash	
tack		mash	

1. Did the little boy [hash / dash / mash] into the  ?

2. I have a [mash / dash / rash] on my hand.

3. Jack will [pack / rack / back] the bags for you.

4. Did the  [stash / crash / trash] into the  ?

5. The cat sat on the [track / lack / black] .

6. I will give you [splash / cash / clash] for that.

7. Can I have a little [snack / back] ?

Name _____   Date _____

Trace over the words three or four times. Next, write the word in the space provided.

This side for those who print.   This side for those who use cursive.

ack   *ack*

pack   *pack*

tack   *tack*

Jack   *Jack*

ash   *ash*

cash   *cash*

rash   *rash*

gash   *gash*

Name _____   Date _____

I. Write the name of the picture in the blank.
   Look for the word in the puzzle and draw a line around it.

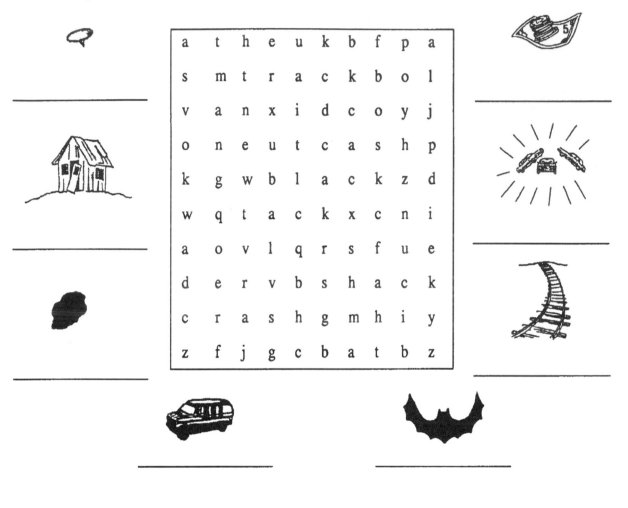

a	t	h	e	u	k	b	f	p	a
s	m	t	r	a	c	k	b	o	l
v	a	n	x	i	d	c	o	y	j
o	n	e	u	t	c	a	s	h	p
k	g	w	b	l	a	c	k	z	d
w	q	t	a	c	k	x	c	n	i
a	o	v	l	q	r	s	f	u	e
d	e	r	v	b	s	h	a	c	k
c	r	a	s	h	g	m	h	i	y
z	f	j	g	c	b	a	t	b	z

© 1993 by Rosella Bernstein

II. Write a rhyming word on the blank line for each word:

back _____

tack _____

cash _____

tag _____

nap _____

Name _____ Date _____

These are difficult multisyllable words at this level. However, explain to the pupil that if he/she can figure out the part that is underlined and use the context clues, it will be less difficult to decode the word. Practice helps.

1. Get a <u>flash</u>light so we can see who it is.   flashlight

2. This <u>crack</u>er is a good snack.   cracker

3. My 👟👟 are in the blue <u>pack</u>age.   package

4. I will make a <u>Jack</u>-O'-Lantern from this 🎃.   Jack-O'-Lantern

5. The 🏈 can run and <u>tack</u>le.   tackle

6. I like to *abcdefg* on the <u>black</u>board.   blackboard

7. My 📖📖 are in my <u>back</u>pack.   backpack

For 2 players. Use a spinning wheel that has numerals 1–6 on it. The pupil advances the number of spaces if he/she says the words correctly.

gash	crash	crack	snack	black	gap	rash	STOP

fan

back	mash	trash	tack	flash	flat	glad

cap

GO	pack	flag	Jack	pan	lap	cash	sack

Name _____   Date _____

1. Explain to the pupil that all the pictures on this page begin with the same sound as the word *apple*.
2. Read the following definitions to the pupil as you point to the picture:
   a. An antelope looks like a deer. It usually has a single pair of horns.
   b. An ax is a sharp tool for chopping things like trees, wood, and ice.
3. Next, the pupil names each picture and writes the name from the list.

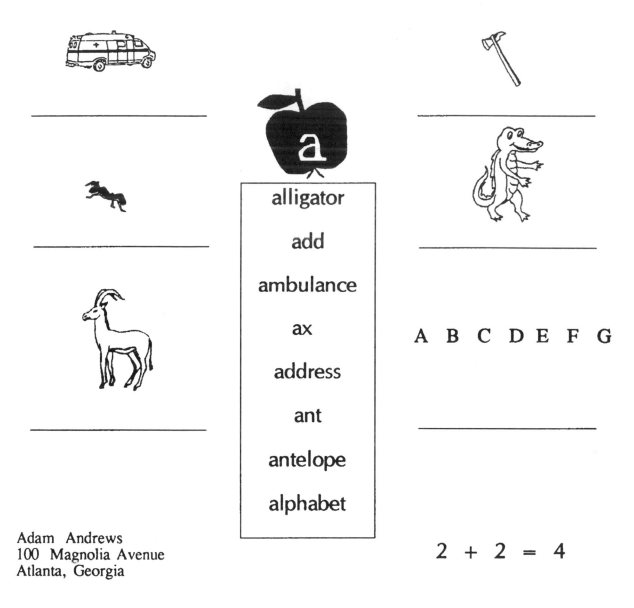

alligator

add

ambulance

ax

address

ant

antelope

alphabet

A B C D E F G

Adam Andrews
100 Magnolia Avenue
Atlanta, Georgia

2 + 2 = 4

CHECK LIST

ă

bag	cap	Dad	fan	gap
bat	can	Dan	fat	gash
bad	cat	dam		
ban	cash	dash		
back				

ham	Jan	lag	map	nap
had	jam	lap	man	
hat	Jack	lack	mad	
hash		lash	mat	
			mash	

pan	rag	sap	tag	van
Pam	rap	Sam	tap	
pad	ran	sad	tan	
pat	rack	sack	tack	
pack	rash	sash		
	rat	sat		

wag

Select a word and have the pupil attempt to read it. (Don't select more than a total of ten words a session.) If the pupil is able to read the word, put a plus (+) mark in front of the word. If the pupil is not able to read the word, put a minus (-) mark and change it into a plus when the pupil can recognize it. Make flash cards of the unsuccessful words for practice.

Name _____   Date _____

1. Have the pupil go over the list of words at the top of the exercise.
   Point out to the pupil that the ending of each word is the same.   Examples: *came*   *game*   *tame*.
2. Next have the pupil do the exercise, crossing out the two words that are incorrect.
3. When all the sentences have been done in this way, the pupil returns to the first sentence and *orally* reads each sentence with the correct word.

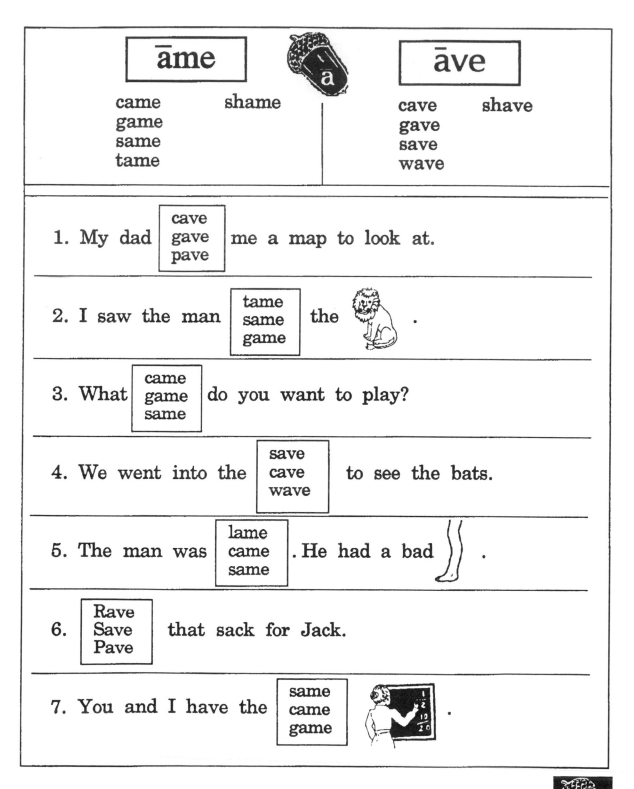

āme		āve	
came	shame	cave	shave
game		gave	
same		save	
tame		wave	

1. My dad | cave / gave / pave | me a map to look at.

2. I saw the man | tame / same / game | the [lion].

3. What | came / game / same | do you want to play?

4. We went into the | save / cave / wave | to see the bats.

5. The man was | lame / came / same |. He had a bad [leg].

6. | Rave / Save / Pave | that sack for Jack.

7. You and I have the | same / came / game | [blackboard].

Name _____   Date _____

Trace over the word three or four times. Next, write the word in the space provided.

This side for those who print.   This side for those who use cursive.

ame   *ame*

same   *same*

tame   *tame*

came   *came*

ave   *ave*

rave   *rave*

wave   *wave*

gave   *gave*

I. Write the name of the picture in the blank.
   Look for the word in the puzzle and draw a line around it.

a	c	f	e	h	j	v	q	r	o	z
j	t	a	p	e	j	t	m	d	i	e
d	a	f	i	n	a	c	i	h	q	o
p	c	b	w	l	w	a	v	e	n	t
v	k	u	p	j	o	v	y	w	h	e
c	g	d	f	b	k	e	k	s	o	k
h	m	l	g	z	y	i	g	x	g	y
v	m	c	a	s	h	s	v	l	t	u
f	i	r	m	u	r	n	d	b	t	x
s	e	j	e	w	u	q	w	a	g	h
q	k	s	x	c	b	h	k	o	f	p
r	f	l	a	g	l	s	a	c	k	e
a	y	w	z	m	a	p	c	n	d	z

II. If the first vowel in the word has the short sound (as in apple), mark the word like this: **săck.**

If the first vowel in the word has the long sound (as in acorn), mark the word like this: **sāve.**

1. same
2. back
3. game
4. cash
5. gave

6. cave
7. came
8. nag
9. save
10. cat

11. lap
12. wave
13. glad
14. ham
15. tame

Name _____   Date _____

I. Read the first two sentences. Fill in the missing word in the last sentence.

    1. I like to play the game of tag.

    2. You like to play the game of tag.

    3. We like to play the _____ of tag.

---

    1. Is the 🦁 tame?

    2. Is the 🐯 tame?

    3. Are they _____ ?

---

    1. Bats are in the cave.

    2. 🐍 🐍 are in the cave.

    3. Bats and 🐍 🐍 are in the _____ .

II.

DOWN ↓

1. [gas pump]
2. [dog]
4. [face]
6. [mole]
8. [map of U.S.]
10. [envelope]
11. [cat]

ACROSS →

1. [crossword]
3. [crying face]
5. [eraser]
7. [shell]
9. [person with dog]
11. [cap]
12. 10

25

Name _____   Date _____

1. Point out to the pupil that the ending of each word is the same. Examples: n*ail* p*ail* s*ail*.
2. Next have the pupil do the exercise, filling in the letter that makes sense.
3. When all the sentences have been done this way, the pupil returns to the sentence and *orally* reads each sentence with the correct word.

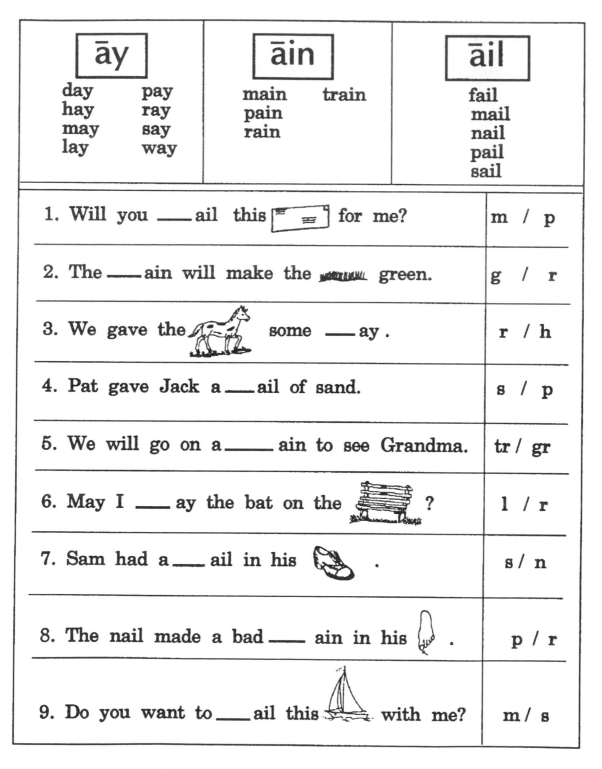

$\overline{a}y$	$\overline{a}in$	$\overline{a}il$
day pay	main train	fail
hay ray	pain	mail
may say	rain	nail
lay way		pail
		sail

1. Will you ___ ail this [envelope] for me?	m / p
2. The ___ ain will make the grass green.	g / r
3. We gave the [horse] some ___ ay .	r / h
4. Pat gave Jack a ___ ail of sand.	s / p
5. We will go on a ___ ain to see Grandma.	tr / gr
6. May I ___ ay the bat on the [bench] ?	l / r
7. Sam had a ___ ail in his [shoe] .	s / n
8. The nail made a bad ___ ain in his [foot] .	p / r
9. Do you want to ___ ail this [sailboat] with me?	m / s

26

Trace over the word three or four times. Next, write the word in the space provided.

This side for those who print.   This side for those who use cursive.

ai   ail

sail   sail

pail   pail

jail   jail

ay   ay

may   may

say   say

way   way

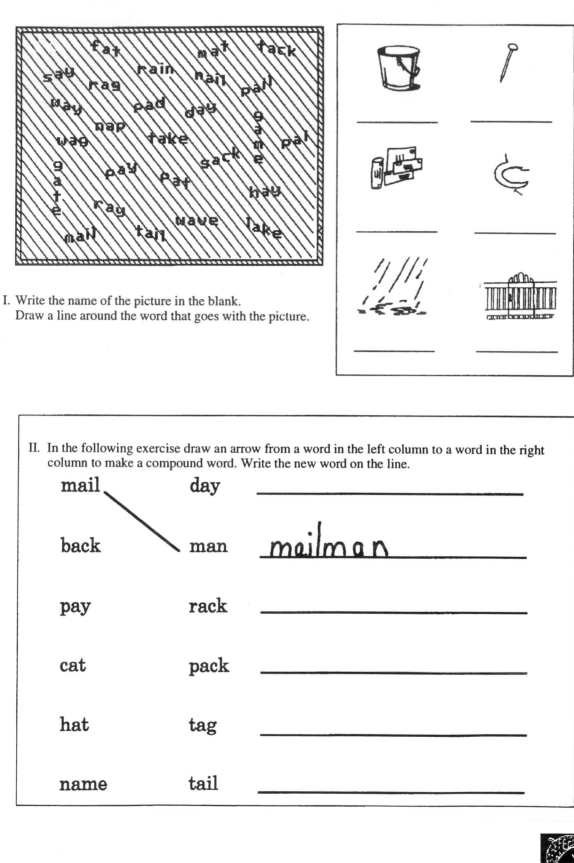

I. Write the name of the picture in the blank.
   Draw a line around the word that goes with the picture.

II. In the following exercise draw an arrow from a word in the left column to a word in the right column to make a compound word. Write the new word on the line.

mail   day   _____

back   man   *mailman* _____

pay   rack   _____

cat   pack   _____

hat   tag   _____

name   tail   _____

I. Mark the vowel in each word either long or short. The row with all the long *a* words is BINGO.

pain	mad	pay	tame	bat
hay	rain	cane	save	gave
day	pave	**ā**	may	tag
cap	paid	flap	flag	crack
cave	pack	glad	cash	fan

II. Decide if the picture at the beginning of each line has a long *a* or a short *a* sound. Write in the blank. Then draw a line around the word that rhymes and has the same vowel sound. The first one is done for you.

ā	dad	make	(pail)	rat
	tag	paid	May	cash
	fan	map	mail	say
	day	bat	rain	tag
	fail	ran	pan	pain

29

Name _____   Date _____

1. Have the pupil go over the lists of words at the top of the exercise.
   Point out to the pupil that the ending of each word is the same. Examples: *face race* p*lace*.
2. Next have the student do the exercise, crossing out the two words that are incorrect.
3. When all the sentences have been done this way, the pupil goes back to the first sentence and *orally* reads each sentence with the correct word.

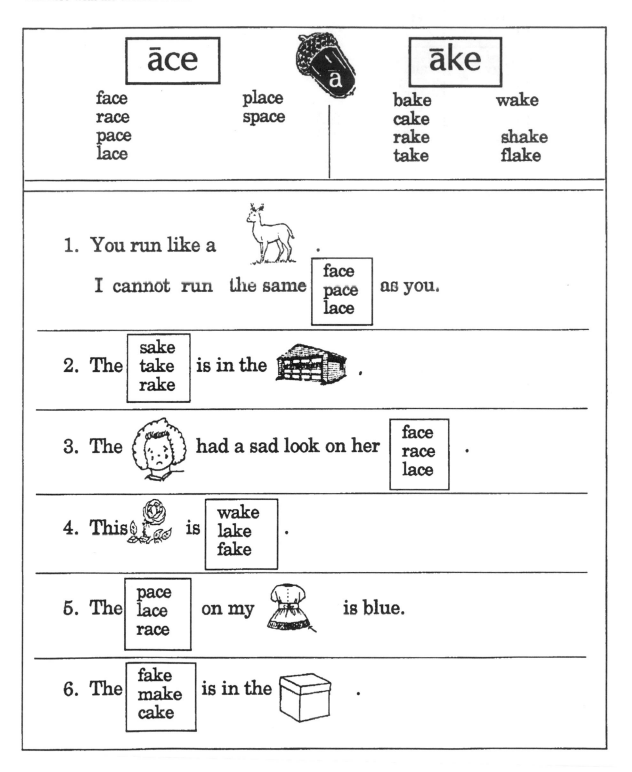

āce		āke	
face	place	bake	wake
race	space	cake	
pace		rake	shake
lace		take	flake

1. You run like a ⟨deer⟩.
   I cannot run the same | face / pace / lace | as you.

2. The | sake / take / rake | is in the ⟨barn⟩.

3. The ⟨girl⟩ had a sad look on her | face / race / lace |.

4. This ⟨rose⟩ is | wake / lake / fake |.

5. The | pace / lace / race | on my ⟨dress⟩ is blue.

6. The | fake / make / cake | is in the ⟨box⟩.

Name _____   Date _____

Trace over the word three or four times. Next, write the word in the space provided.

This side for those who print.   This side for those who use cursive.

ace   *ace*

race   *race*

face   *face*

pace   *pace*

ake   *ake*

bake   *bake*

take   *take*

make   *make*

Name _____   Date _____

I. Put a line around the words that go with the picture.

A.	1. A race on a lake? 2. A race into space?	
B.	1. A sad face? 2. A glad face?	
C.	1. A rake and a pail? 2. A rake and a pal?	
D.	1. A hat and a cap? 2. A hat and a cape?	
E.	1. Rain on the pan? 2. Rain on the pane?	

II.

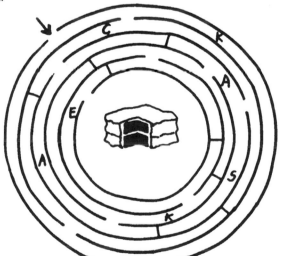

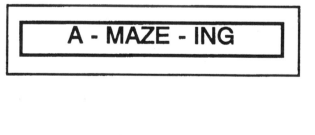

A - MAZE - ING

___ ___ ___ ___ ___

Name _____   Date _____

CHECK LIST
ā

bake	cake	day	face	gain
bail	cave		fake	gave
	cane		fame	game
			fade	

hay	Jake	lake	main	nail
	jail	lay	mail	name
	Jay	lace	mace	
		lame	make	
			made	
			may	

pail	rain	same	take	wake
pain	rail	save	tame	wave
pace	rake	sake	tail	way
pave	race	sail		
pay	rave	say		
	ray			

Select a word and have the pupil attempt to read it. (Don't select more than a total of ten words at a session.)
If the pupil is able to read the word, put a plus (+) mark in front of the word.
If he/she is not able to read the word, put a minus (-) mark in front of the word.
Make flash cards of the unsuccessful words for practice.

33

Name _____   Date _____

1. Have the pupil go over the lists of words at the top of the exercise. Point out to the pupil that the ending of each word is the same. Examples: h*en*   m*en*   p*en*.
2. Next have the pupil do the exercise, crossing out the two words that are incorrect.
3. When all the sentences have been done this way, the pupil returns to the first sentence and *orally* reads each sentence with the correct word.

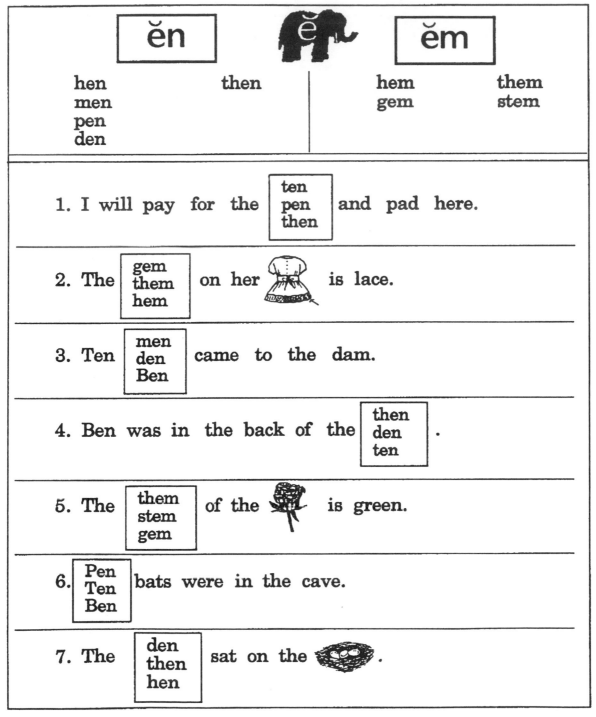

ĕn		ĕm	
hen	then	hem	them
men		gem	stem
pen			
den			

1. I will pay for the
   | ten |
   | pen |
   | then |
   and pad here.

2. The
   | gem |
   | them |
   | hem |
   on her 👗 is lace.

3. Ten
   | men |
   | den |
   | Ben |
   came to the dam.

4. Ben was in the back of the
   | then |
   | den |
   | ten |
   .

5. The
   | them |
   | stem |
   | gem |
   of the 🌹 is green.

6.
   | Pen |
   | Ten |
   | Ben |
   bats were in the cave.

7. The
   | den |
   | then |
   | hen |
   sat on the 🪺 .

Name _____   Date _____

Trace over the word three or four times. Next, write the word in the space provided.

This side for those who print.   This side for those who use cursive.

en   *en*

men   *men*

den   *den*

pen   *pen*

em   *em*

gem   *gem*

them   *them*

stem   *stem*

Name _____ Date _____

I.

ACROSS →

DOWN ↓

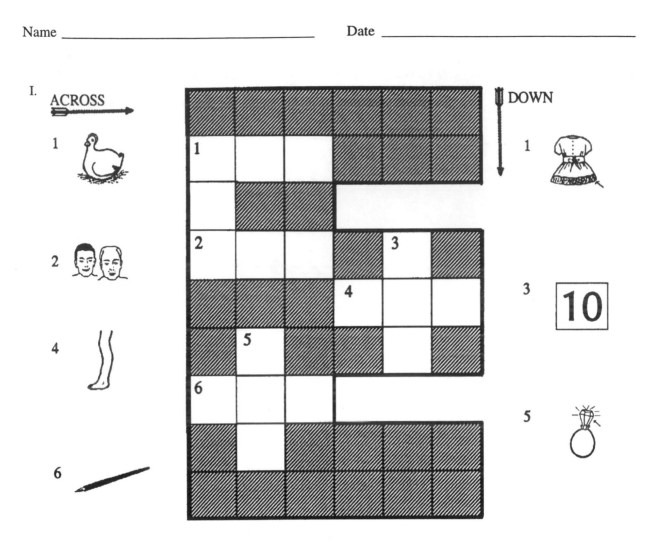

1

2

3 $\boxed{10}$

4

5

6

II. Draw a line around the words that go with the picture.

old man old men		a black pan a black pen	
a hen a hand		bag beg	
bait bat		ham hem	

Name _____   Date _____

This exercise is designed to help the student try to decode multisyllable words using the basic skills learned in this lesson plus context clues. The pupil is not expected to be able to read the multisyllable words the first time around. Practice helps.

1. I have a bad 👄 .
   I will go to the <u>den</u>tist.   dentist

2. I will ✍ my name with this <u>pen</u>cil.   pencil

3. This ham is very <u>ten</u>der.   tender

4. Look at a map.

   Can you see <u>Penn</u>sylvania?   Pennsylvania

   Can you see <u>Ken</u>tucky?   Kentucky

5. We saw some <u>pen</u>guins at the 🦒🐘 .   penguins

6. I will pay you a <u>pen</u>ny for that 🍎 .   penny

Fill in the vowel letter:

h __ n		t __ g	
r __ t		c __ ke	
st __ m		p __ n	
m __ n		c __ p	

37

Name _____   Date _____

1. Have the pupil go over the lists of words at the top of the exercise. Point out to the pupil that the ending of each word is the same. Examples: b*ell*   f*ell*   s*ell*.
2. Next have the pupil do the exercise, crossing out the two words that are incorrect.
3. When all the sentences have been done this way, the pupil returns to the first sentence and *orally* reads each sentence with the correct word.

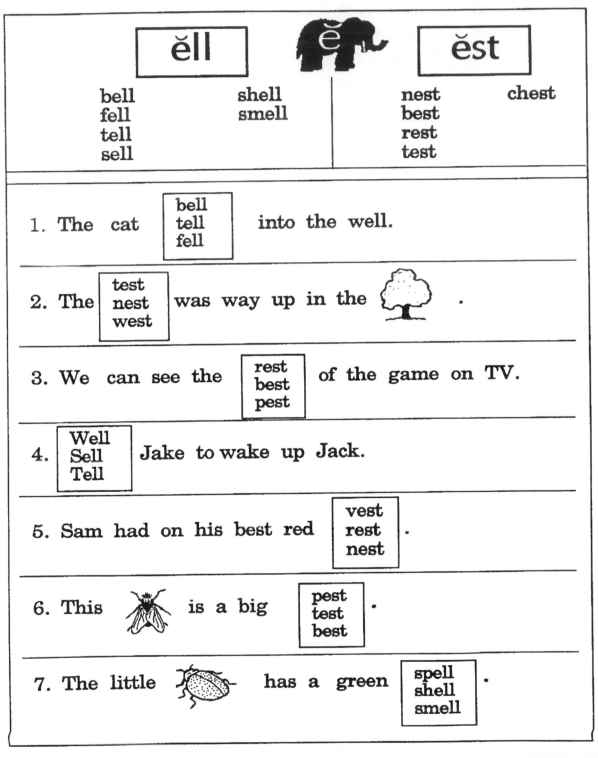

ĕll   **ĕ**   **ĕst**

bell	shell		nest	chest
fell	smell		best	
tell			rest	
sell			test	

1. The cat [bell / tell / fell] into the well.

2. The [test / nest / west] was way up in the 🌳 .

3. We can see the [rest / best / pest] of the game on TV.

4. [Well / Sell / Tell] Jake to wake up Jack.

5. Sam had on his best red [vest / rest / nest] .

6. This 🪰 is a big [pest / test / best] .

7. The little 🐞 has a green [spell / shell / smell] .

Name _____   Date _____

Trace over the word three or four times. Next, write the word in the space provided.

This side for those who print   This side for those who use cursive.

ell   *ell*

fell   *fell*

yell   *yell*

sell   *sell*

est   *est*

pest   *pest*

rest   *rest*

test   *test*

39

I. Write the name of the picture in the blank.
   Look for the word in the puzzle. Draw a line around it.

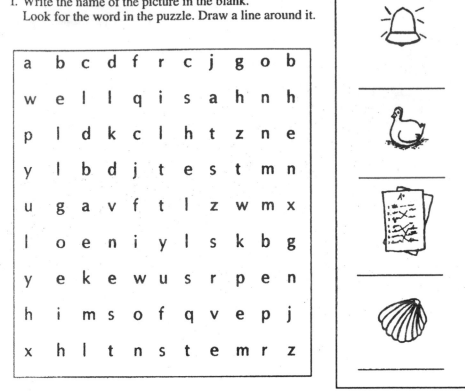

a	b	c	d	f	r	c	j	g	o	b
w	e	l	l	q	i	s	a	h	n	h
p	l	d	k	c	l	h	t	z	n	e
y	l	b	d	j	t	e	s	t	m	n
u	g	a	v	f	t	l	z	w	m	x
l	o	e	n	i	y	l	s	k	b	g
y	e	k	e	w	u	s	r	p	e	n
h	i	m	s	o	f	q	v	e	p	j
x	h	l	t	n	s	t	e	m	r	z

II. Draw a line around the word that names the picture.

shall		vest	
shell		vast	
ball		pail	
bell		pal	
cap		beg	
cape		bag	
nest		pest	
net		past	

40

Name _____   Date _____

I. Fill in the initial missing consonant in each sentence. Then read the sentence again.

1. The 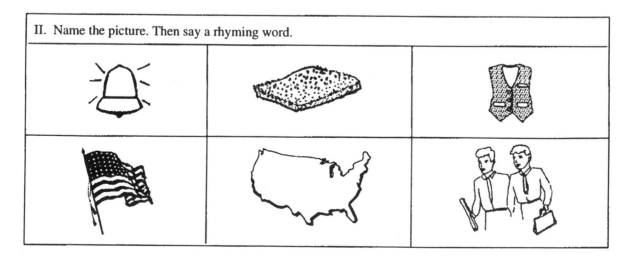 made a __ est out of hay.   n   r   b

2. I got a B+ on the __ est.   b   r   t

3. Jack had on a red and blue __ est.   t   v   p

4. We can stop and __ est here.   p   b   r

5. This is the __ est that I can do.   r   t   b

6. The little boy __ ell out of the bed.   f   w   b

7. Dan will __ ell the rake to you for $1.   w   s   f

8. Do not __ ell at the little   b   w   y

9. Did Sam look down into the __ ell?   w   f   s

II. Name the picture. Then say a rhyming word.		

41

Name _____ Date _____

1. Have the pupil go over the list of words at the top of the exercise. Point out to the student that the ending of each word is the same. Examples: b*ed*   r*ed*   sl*ed*.
2. Next have the pupil do the exercise, crossing out the two words that are incorrect.
3. When all the sentences have been done this way, the pupil returns to the first sentence and *orally* reads each sentence with the correct word.

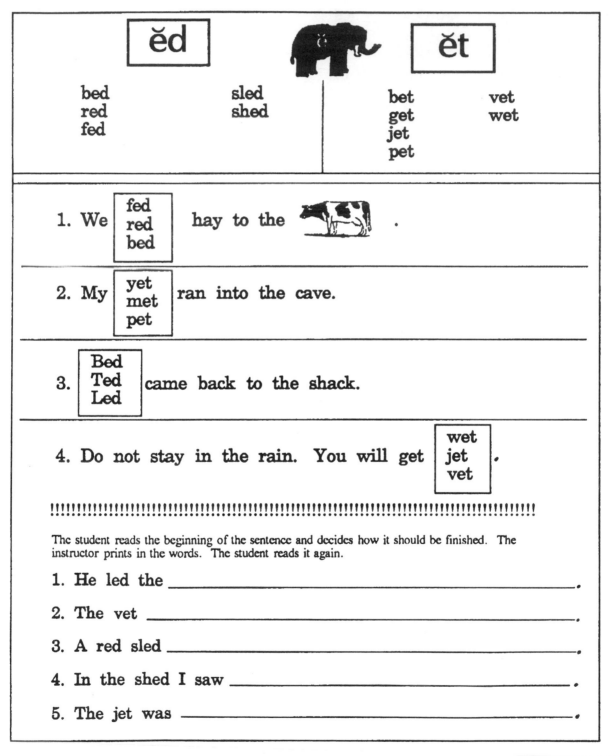

ĕd		ĕt

bed   sled   bet   vet
red   shed   get   wet
fed   jet
                                   pet

1. We | fed / red / bed | hay to the  .

2. My | yet / met / pet | ran into the cave.

3. | Bed / Ted / Led | came back to the shack.

4. Do not stay in the rain. You will get | wet / jet / vet | .

!!!

The student reads the beginning of the sentence and decides how it should be finished. The instructor prints in the words. The student reads it again.

1. He led the _____ .

2. The vet _____ .

3. A red sled _____ .

4. In the shed I saw _____ .

5. The jet was _____ .

42

Name _____   Date _____

Trace over the word three or four times. Next, write the word in the space provided.

This side for those who print.   This side for those who use cursive.

ed   *ed*

red   *red*

fed   *fed*

led   *led*

et   *et*

jet   *jet*

vet   *vet*

wet   *wet*

© 1993 by Rosella Bernstein

43

Name _____ Date _____

I.

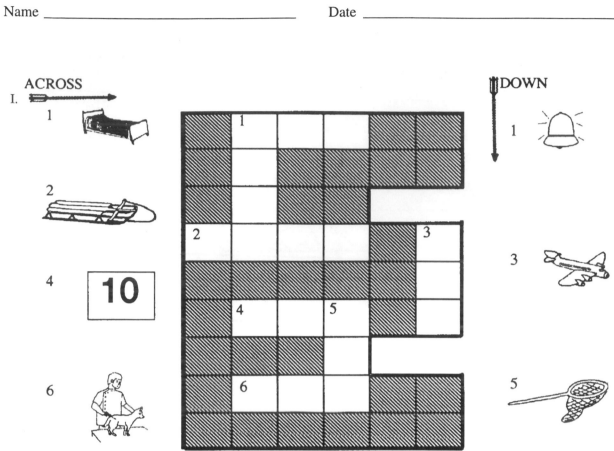

ACROSS

1 (bed)

2 (sled)

4 **10**

6 (boy with fox/pet)

DOWN

1 (bell)

3 (plane)

5 (net)

II. Put a line around the word or words in each line that has the same vowel sound as the picture on the left.

ă (apple)	ham	tail	cash	Dad	pave
ā (gorilla)	hash	May	pain	race	lap
ĕ (elephant)	bed	test	see	she	jet

Name _____   Date _____

These are difficult multisyllable words at this level. However, explain to the pupil that if he/she can figure out the part that is underlined and use the context clues, it will be less difficult to decode the word. Practice helps.

1. Ted will mail the <u>let</u>ter for me.   letter

2. We have good <u>let</u>tuce in the ⬚ .   lettuce

3. I can see the game <u>bet</u>ter from up here.   better

4. The <u>ped</u>al is not on the 🚲 .   pedal

5. He ran the best in the race.

   They gave him a <u>med</u>al.   medal

6. Jenny is 🛏 .

   She will take <u>med</u>icine to get better.   medicine

For 2 players. Use a spinning wheel that has numerals 1–6 on it. The pupil advances the number of spaces if he/she says the words correctly.

bed	best	bell	sled	ten	test	hen	S T O P

pen	well	west	yell	wet	smell	vest	shell	fell

G O	jet	pet	nest	set	red	men	met	leg	den

45

Name _____ Date _____

1. Have the pupil go over the lists of words at the top of the exercise. Point out to the pupil that the ending of each word is the same. Examples: n*eck*   d*eck*   ch*eck*.
2. Next have the pupil do the exercises, crossing out the two words that are incorrect.
3. When all the sentences have been done this way, the pupil returns to the first sentence and *orally* reads each sentence with the correct word.

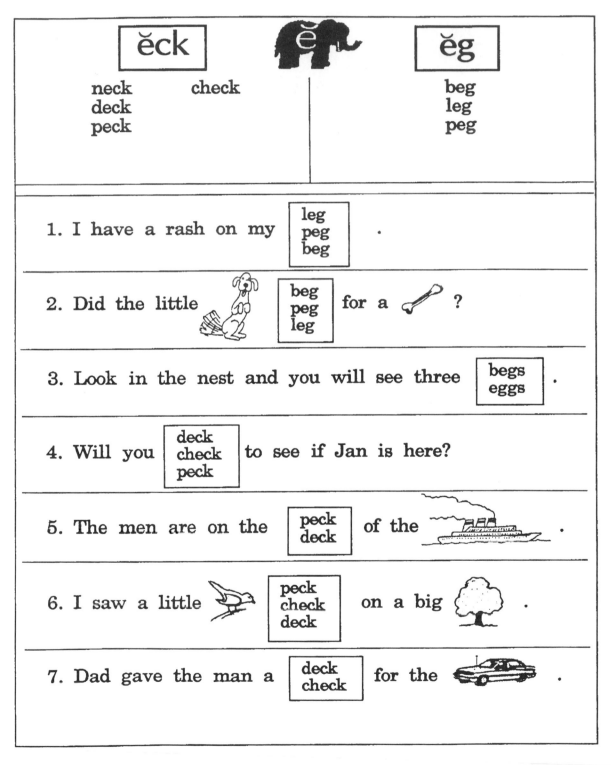

ĕck	ĕ	ĕg

neck   check
deck
peck

beg
leg
peg

1. I have a rash on my [leg / peg / beg] .

2. Did the little 🐕 [beg / peg / leg] for a 🦴 ?

3. Look in the nest and you will see three [begs / eggs] .

4. Will you [deck / check / peck] to see if Jan is here?

5. The men are on the [peck / deck] of the 🚢 .

6. I saw a little 🐦 [peck / check / deck] on a big 🌳 .

7. Dad gave the man a [deck / check] for the 🚗 .

Trace over the word three or four times. Next, write the word in the space provided.

This side for those who print.   This side for those who use cursive.

eck   *eck*

deck   *deck*

peck   *peck*

check   *check*

eg   *eg*

leg   *leg*

keg   *keg*

egg   *egg*

Name _____ Date _____

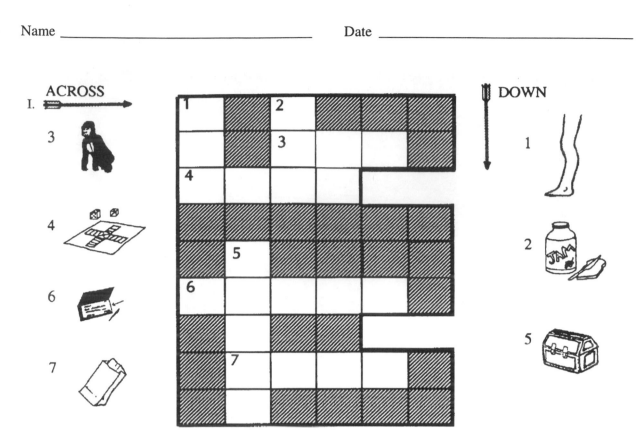

I. ACROSS →

3

4

6

7

DOWN ↓

1

2

5

II. Write the vowel in the blank to complete the word.

c__ ke		n__st	
p__n		f__ce	
b__ll		l__g	
m__p		b__t	
s__ck		n__ck	

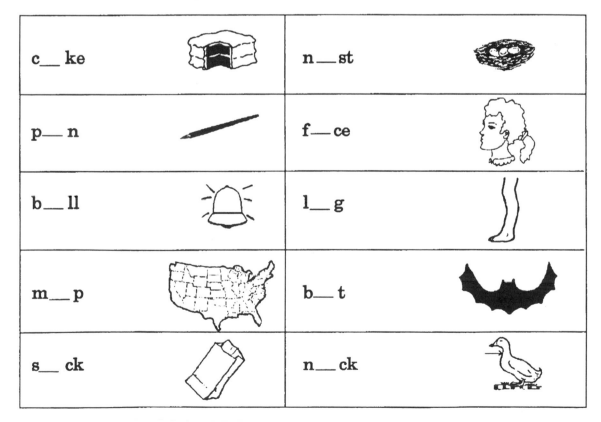

 ĕ

Name _____   Date _____

These are difficult multisyllable words at this level. However, explain to the pupil that if he/she can figure out the part that is underlined (mostly words learned in this lesson) and also use the context clues, it will be less difficult to decode the word. Practice helps.

1. The game of <u>check</u>ers is fun to play.   checkers

2. Did the <u>beg</u>gar ask you for some 🪙 ?   beggar
   He had no cash at all.

3. The <u>neck</u>lace around her neck is blue.   necklace

4. I cannot pay for this rake.

   I do not have my <u>check</u>book with me.   checkbook

5. I gave my dad a <u>neck</u>tie for Christmas.   necktie

Put a line around the picture that rhymes with the word at the left of each line.

pen				
deck				
nest				
let				
tell				

49

Name _____   Date _____

1. Explain to the pupil that all pictures on this page begin with the same vowel sound as the word *elephant*.
2. Read the following definitions to the pupil as you point to each picture:
   a. An elk is a large deer. It has spreading antlers that are shed once a year. New antlers grow back during the next year.
   b. An excavator digs or scoops out large amounts of dirt from the ground and loads it into trucks.
   c. An elf is a tiny, playful fairy.
3. Next, the pupil names each picture and writes the name from the list.

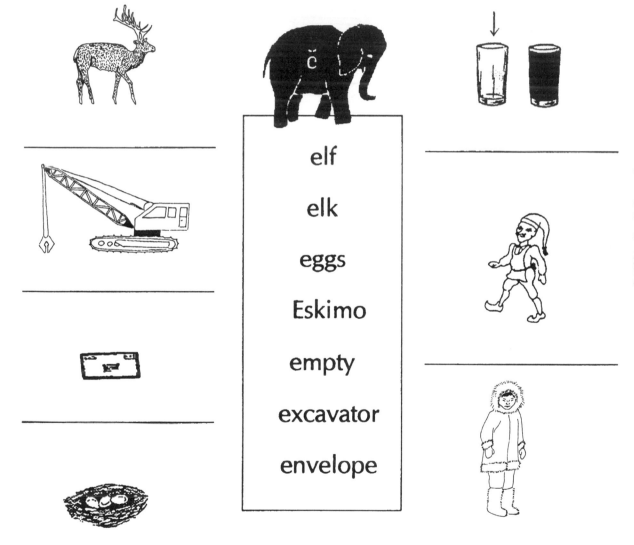

elf

elk

eggs

Eskimo

empty

excavator

envelope

Name _____   Date _____

CHECK LIST

$$\breve{e}$$

bell	deck	fell	get	hen
best	den	fed		hem
beg				
bet				
bed				

jet	keg	leg	met	nest
		let	men	net
		led		neck

peck	red	set	ten	vet
pest	rest	sell	tell	vest
peg			test	
pet			Ted	
pen				

wet	yen
west	yet
well	yell

Select a word and have the pupil attempt to read it. (Don't select more than a total of ten words a session.)
If the pupil is able to read the word, put a plus (+) mark in front of the word.
If the pupil is not able to read the word, put a minus (-) mark and change it into a plus when the pupil can recognize it.
Make flash cards of the unsuccessful words for practice.

Name _____   Date _____

1. Have the pupil go over the lists of words at the top of the exercise. Point out to the pupil that the ending of each word is the same. Examples: f*eed*   w*eed*   s*eed*.
2. Next have the pupil do the exercise, crossing out the two words that are incorrect.
3. When all the sentences have been done in this way, the pupil returns to the first sentence and *orally* reads each sentence with the correct word.

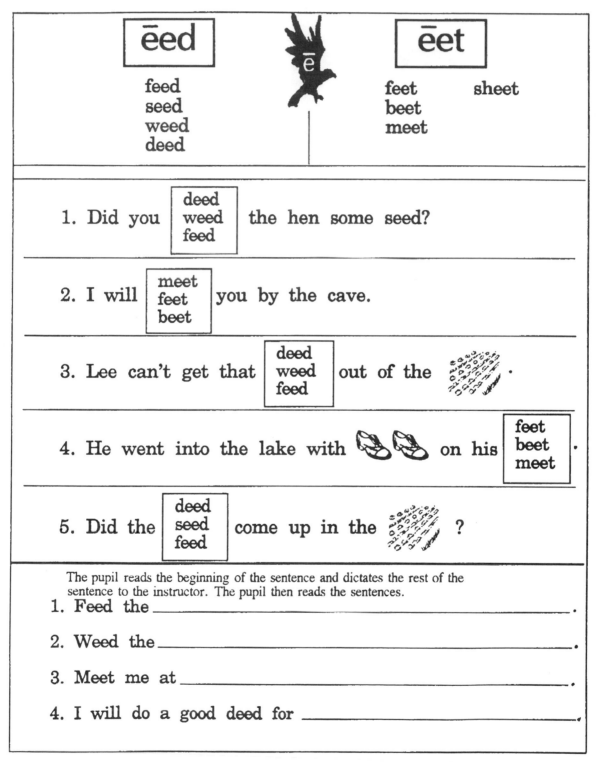

ēed

feed
seed
weed
deed

ēet

feet   sheet
beet
meet

1. Did you | deed / weed / feed | the hen some seed?

2. I will | meet / feet / beet | you by the cave.

3. Lee can't get that | deed / weed / feed | out of the ⬚ .

4. He went into the lake with 👞👞 on his | feet / beet / meet |.

5. Did the | deed / seed / feed | come up in the ⬚ ?

The pupil reads the beginning of the sentence and dictates the rest of the sentence to the instructor. The pupil then reads the sentences.

1. Feed the _____ .

2. Weed the _____ .

3. Meet me at _____ .

4. I will do a good deed for _____ .

Name _____   Date _____

Trace over the word three or four times. Next, write the word in the space provided.

This side for those who print.   This side for those who use cursive.

eed   *eed*

feed   *feed*

seed   *seed*

weed   *weed*

eet   *eet*

feet   *feet*

meet   *meet*

beet   *beet*

53

Name _____   Date _____

I. Draw a line around the group of words that goes with the picture.

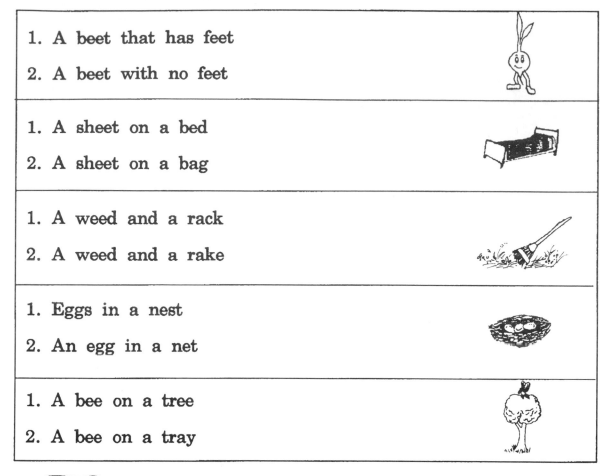

1. A beet that has feet

2. A beet with no feet

1. A sheet on a bed

2. A sheet on a bag

1. A weed and a rack

2. A weed and a rake

1. Eggs in a nest

2. An egg in a net

1. A bee on a tree

2. A bee on a tray

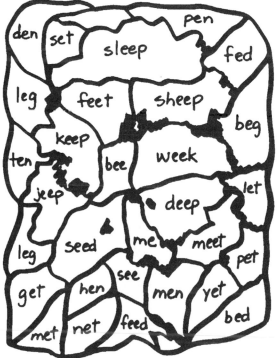

den set sleep pen fed
leg feet sheep beg
keep week
ten bee
jeep deep let
leg seed me meet pet
get hen see men yet
met net feed bed

	PICTURE SHOW	

— — — — —

II. Color green all the sections that have long e words.

54

1. I will meet Pam at the .

   You will meet Pam at the _____ .

   What will we do?   _____ Pam at the _____

2. I will do a good deed.

   You will do a good deed.

   What will we do?   A good _____

3. Jan will rake the seed into the _____ .

   Dan will rake the seed into the _____ .

   What will they rake into the _____ ? _____

4. He will feed the _____

   She will feed the _____

   What will they do?   _____ the _____

5. The weed is yellow.

   The weed is green.

   What is yellow and green?   The _____

6. I see a big bed.

   A green sheet is on the bed.

   What is on the bed?   A green _____

Name _____   Date _____

1. Have the pupil go over the list of words at the top of the exercise. Point out to the pupil that the ending of each word is the same. Examples: d*eep*   j*eep*   sl*eep*.
2. Next have the pupil do the exercises, crossing out the two words that are incorrect.
3. When all the sentences have been done in this way, the pupil returns to the first sentence and *orally* reads each sentence with the correct word.

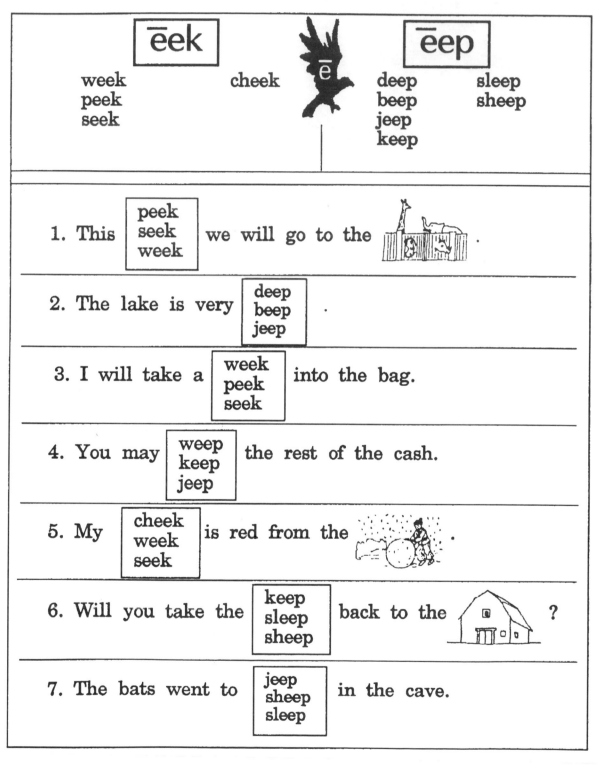

ēek

week   cheek   ē   deep   sleep
peek   beep   sheep
seek   jeep
                          keep

1. This | peek / seek / week | we will go to the [giraffe/zoo].

2. The lake is very | deep / beep / jeep | .

3. I will take a | week / peek / seek | into the bag.

4. You may | weep / keep / jeep | the rest of the cash.

5. My | cheek / week / seek | is red from the [snow scene].

6. Will you take the | keep / sleep / sheep | back to the [barn]?

7. The bats went to | jeep / sheep / sleep | in the cave.

Name _____   Date _____

Trace over the word three or four times. Next, write the word in the space provided.

This side for those who print.   This side for those who use cursive.

eek   *eek*

week   *week*

peek   *peek*

cheek   *cheek*

eep   *eep*

deep   *deep*

jeep   *jeep*

sleep   *sleep*

Put a line around the picture that goes with the sentence.

1. It can say "peep peep."

2. A week is on this.

3. It can go "beep beep."

4. It is very deep.

5. This is a jeep.

6. He has jam on his cheek.

7. It can say, "Baa, Baa."

Name _____   Date _____

I. Mark the first vowel of each word with a short or long mark. BINGO is all the long *e* words in a single row either down, across, or diagonal.

cheek	weed	test	jeep	deck
feet	bell	net	seed	bet
need	neck	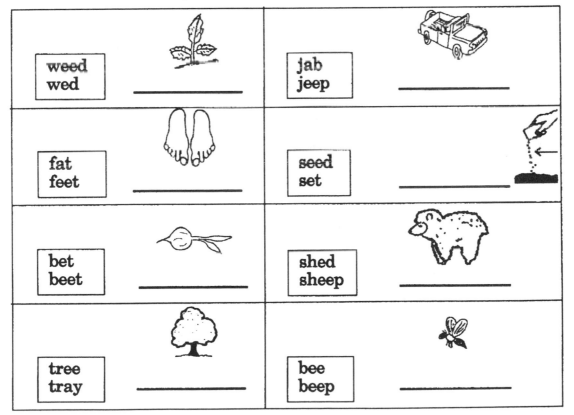	creep	pest
sleep	feed	deep	beet	peek
then	seek	web	let	end

II. Write the correct word under each picture.

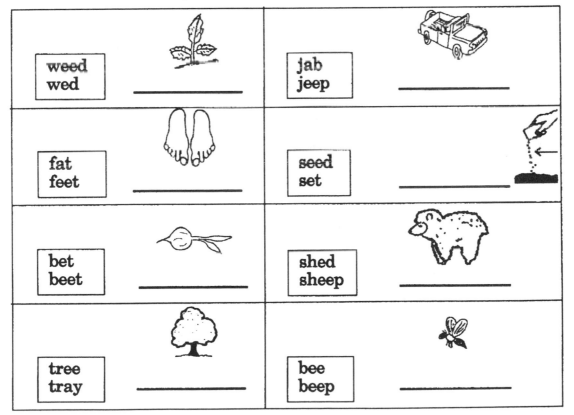

weed
wed
_____

jab
jeep
_____

fat
feet
_____

seed
set
_____

bet
beet
_____

shed
sheep
_____

tree
tray
_____

bee
beep
_____

Name _____ Date _____

1. Have the pupil go over the list of words at the top of the exercise. Point out to the pupil that the ending of each word is the same. Examples: b*eat* h*eat* m*eat*.
2. Next have the student do the exercise, crossing out the two words that are incorrect.
3. When all the sentences have been done in this way, the pupil returns to the first sentence and *orally* reads each sentence with the correct word.

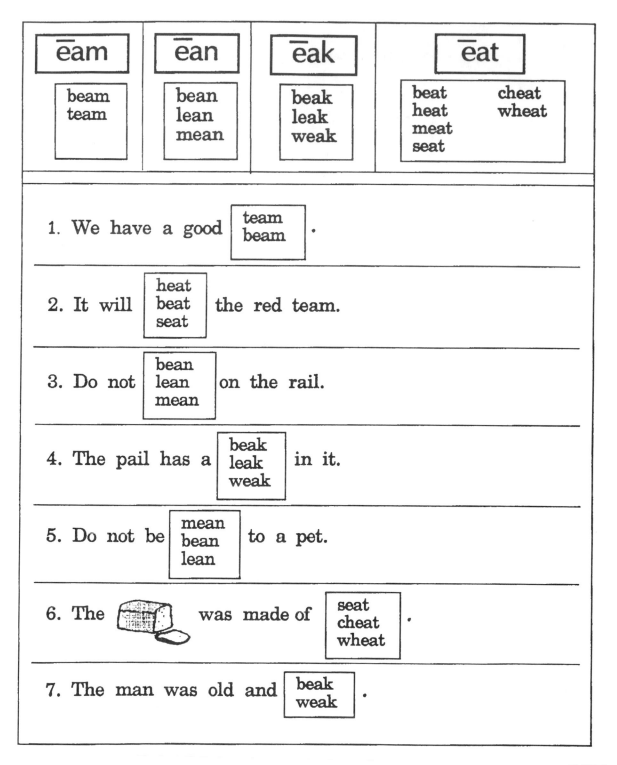

ēam	ēan	ēak	ēat
beam team	bean lean mean	beak leak weak	beat cheat heat wheat meat seat

1. We have a good | team / beam | .

2. It will | heat / beat / seat | the red team.

3. Do not | bean / lean / mean | on the rail.

4. The pail has a | beak / leak / weak | in it.

5. Do not be | mean / bean / lean | to a pet.

6. The [bread] was made of | seat / cheat / wheat | .

7. The man was old and | beak / weak | .

Name _____ Date _____

Trace over the word three or four times. Next, write the word in the space provided.

This side for those who print.   This side for those who use cursive.

eak   *eak*

weak   *weak*

beak   *beak*

leak   *leak*

eat   *eat*

heat   *heat*

beat   *beat*

meat   *meat*

61

I.

1. The best team was here for the race.	
Who was here for the race?	The best_____
2. Pat had a good seat at the race.	
What did Pat have at the race?	A good _____
3. My team beat his team.	
Who beat his team?	My _____
4. The heat at the game made me feel weak.	
What made me feel weak?	The_____
5. We had lean meat to eat.	
What did we have to eat?	Lean _____

II.

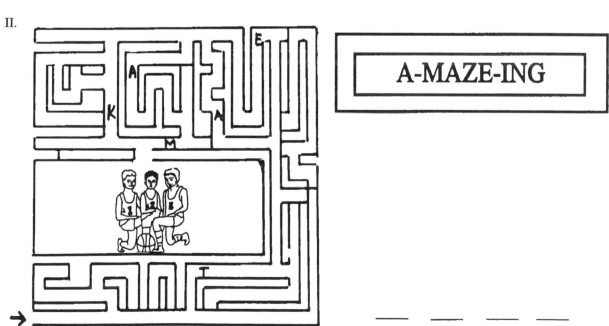

A-MAZE-ING

___ ___ ___ ___ ___

Name _____   Date _____

I. Draw a line around the word that goes with the picture.

met meat		steam stem	
leak lake		ran rain	
wheat wet		seat set	
mean men		cheek check	

II. 1. Explain to the pupil that all the pictures in the exercise below begin with the same vowel sound as the word *eagle*.
   2. Read the following definitions to the pupil as you point to the picture:
      a. An easel is something that holds up a picture or a chalkboard.
      b. An eel is a long slippery fish shaped like a snake.
      c. East is where the sun comes up in the morning.
   3. Next, the pupil names each picture and writes the name from the list.

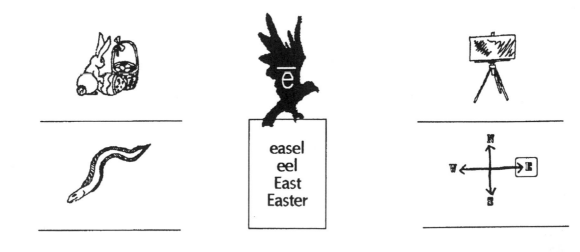

easel
eel
East
Easter

$$\boxed{\overline{ea}} \quad \boxed{\overline{ee}}$$

Practice reading the following sentences:

1. This is a <u>bea</u>gle.   beagle

2. We need a <u>heat</u>er in here.   heater

3. We had ham and <u>bee</u>f to eat.   beef

4. My blue <u>jea</u>ns are old.   jeans

5. A <u>bea</u>ver can eat a ⟶ with its teeth.   beaver

6. The <u>tea</u> bag is in the tea kettle.   tea

7. We went up and down on the <u>see</u>saw.   seesaw

a	b	c	n	x	x	q	c	t	b
b	e	d	e	y	t	r	p	e	c
e	a	e	e	z	r	s	k	e	e
a	l	h	d	n	a	e	z	t	g
v	y	e	l	o	b	e	r	h	i
e	e	a	e	p	e	s	a	r	j
r	m	t	s	q	e	a	s	v	e
h	n	e	t	r	f	w	t	d	a
i	o	r	u	s	b	k	e	x	n
j	b	e	a	g	l	e	r	i	s
k	q	t	b	e	a	v	e	r	z

Look for these words:

beef	jeans
teeth	heater
needle	beaver
seesaw	beagle

HINT: The words may go down or across.

Name _____   Date _____

CHECK LIST

$\overline{e}$

beep	cheek	deed	feed	heel
beet	cheap	deep	feet	heat
beak	cheat			heap
beam				
bean				
beat				

jeep	keep	leap	meet	need
Jean		leak	mean	neat
		lean	meat	

peek	seed	sheep	teen
peep	seek	sheet	team
	seem		
	seep		
	seat		

weed	weak	wheat
week		

Select a word and have the pupil attempt to read it. (Don't select more than a total of ten words a session.)

If the pupil is able to read the word, put a plus (+) mark in front of the word.

If the pupil is not able to read the word, put a minus (-) mark and change it into a plus when the pupil can recognize it.

Make flash cards of the unsuccessful words for practice.

Name _____   Date _____

I. 1. Have the pupil go over the list of words at the top of the exercise. Point out to the pupil that the ending of each word is the same. Examples: b*it*   l*it*   s*it*.
   2. Next have the student do the exercises, crossing out the two words that are incorrect.
   3. When all the sentences have been done in this way, the pupil returns to the first sentence and *orally* reads each sentence with the correct word.

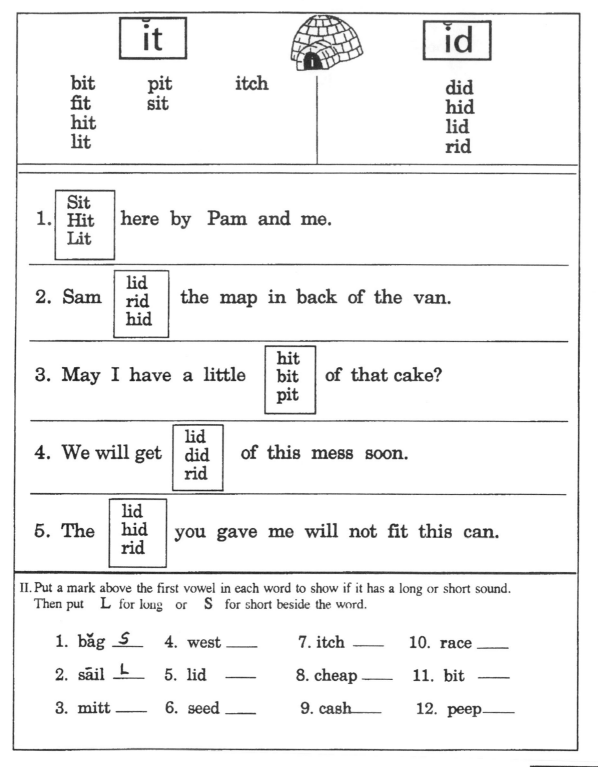

it				id
bit	pit	itch		did
fit	sit			hid
hit				lid
lit				rid

1. | Sit / Hit / Lit | here by Pam and me.

2. Sam | lid / rid / hid | the map in back of the van.

3. May I have a little | hit / bit / pit | of that cake?

4. We will get | lid / did / rid | of this mess soon.

5. The | lid / hid / rid | you gave me will not fit this can.

II. Put a mark above the first vowel in each word to show if it has a long or short sound. Then put   L for long   or   S   for short beside the word.

1. băg _S_   4. west ____   7. itch ____   10. race ____

2. sāil _L_   5. lid ____   8. cheap ____   11. bit ____

3. mitt ____   6. seed ____   9. cash ____   12. peep ____

© 1993 by Rosella Bernstein

Trace over the word three or four times. Next, write the word in the space provided.

This side for those who print.   This side for those who use cursive.

it   *it*

hit   *hit*

sit   *sit*

bit   *bit*

id   *id*

hid   *hid*

lid   *lid*

rid   *rid*

Name _____   Date _____

I. Write a rhyming word for each of the following words:

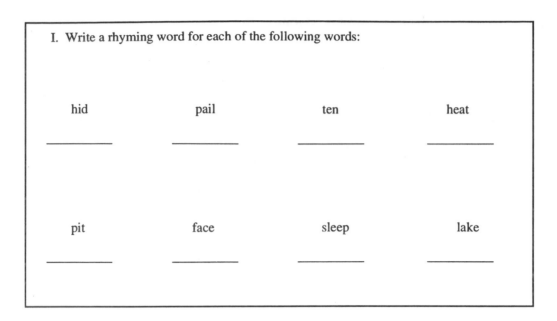

hid   pail   ten   heat

_____   _____   _____   _____

pit   face   sleep   lake

_____   _____   _____   _____

II.

DOT-to-DOT

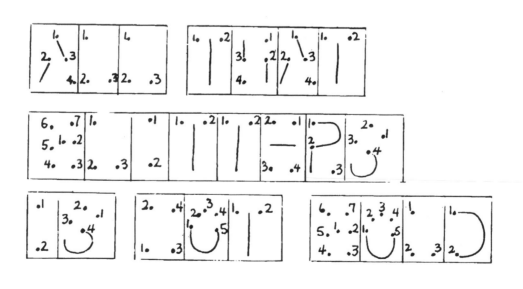

Name _____   Date _____

These are difficult multisyllable words at this level. Explain to the pupil that if he/she can figure out the part that is underlined and use the context clues, it will be less difficult to decode the word. Practice helps.

1. This is not good.

   It is too <u>bit</u>ter.   bitter

---

2. Did the man <u>hit</u>ch the to the ?   hitch

---

3. <u>Pit</u>ch the to me.   pitch

   You are a good <u>pit</u>cher.   pitcher

---

4. Jan is too <u>lit</u>tle to go to the .   little

   She will stay with the <u>sit</u>ter.   sitter

---

5. We will not mess up this place.

   We will not <u>lit</u>ter it.   litter

---

6. Here is a <u>rid</u>dle.   riddle

   What has teeth but cannot eat?

   A .

---

7. Hi <u>Did</u>dle Diddle   diddle

   The Cat and the <u>Fid</u>dle !   fiddle

   The jumped over the .

© 1993 by Rosella Bernstein

Name _____   Date _____

1. Have the pupil go over the lists of words at the top of the exercise. Point out to the pupil that the ending of each word is the same. Examples: b*ig*   d*ig*   p*ig*.
2. Next have the pupil do the exercise, crossing out the two words that are incorrect.
3. When all the sentences have been done in this way, the student goes back to the first sentence and *orally* reads each sentence with the correct word.

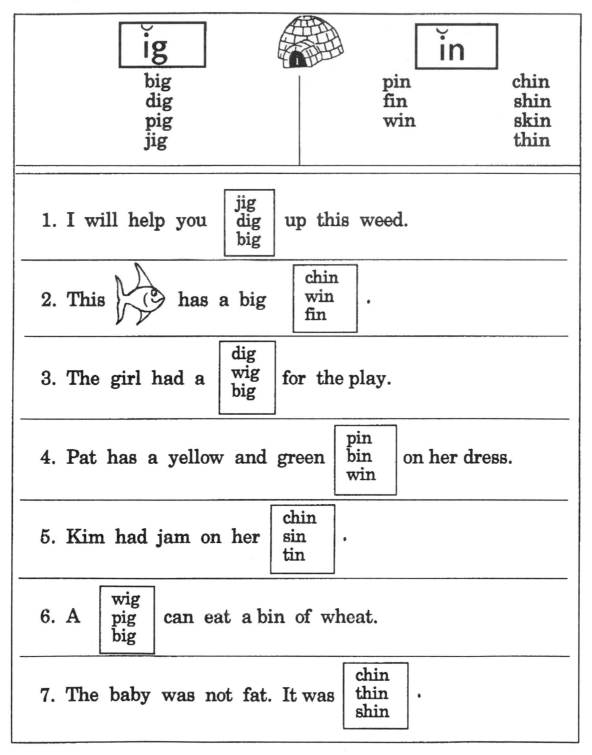

ĭg		ĭn	
big		pin	chin
dig		fin	shin
pig		win	skin
jig			thin

1. I will help you [jig / dig / big] up this weed.

2. This 🐟 has a big [chin / win / fin] .

3. The girl had a [dig / wig / big] for the play.

4. Pat has a yellow and green [pin / bin / win] on her dress.

5. Kim had jam on her [chin / sin / tin] .

6. A [wig / pig / big] can eat a bin of wheat.

7. The baby was not fat. It was [chin / thin / shin] .

Name _____   Date _____

Trace over the word three or four times. Next, write the word in the space provided.

This side for those who print.   This side for those who use cursive.

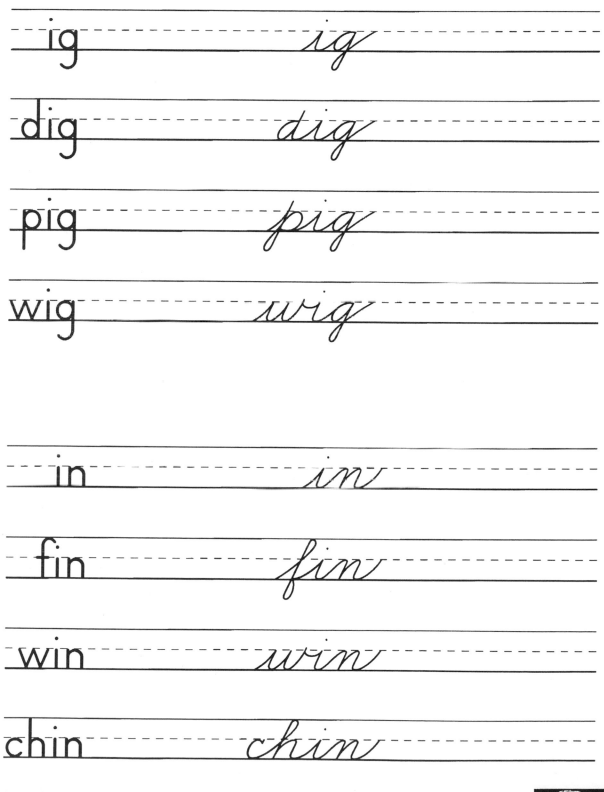

ig   ig

dig   dig

pig   pig

wig   wig

in   in

fin   fin

win   win

chin   chin

Name _____   Date _____

I. Put a circle around the word that names the picture.

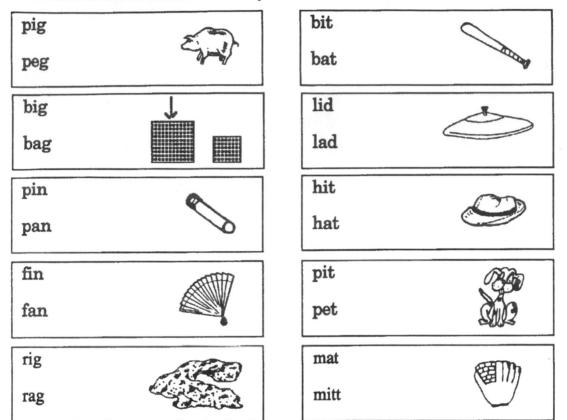

| pig | | bit | |
| peg | | bat | |

| big | | lid | |
| bag | | lad | |

| pin | | hit | |
| pan | | hat | |

| fin | | pit | |
| fan | | pet | |

| rig | | mat | |
| rag | | mitt | |

II. Print the name of the picture in the blank. Find the word in the puzzle.

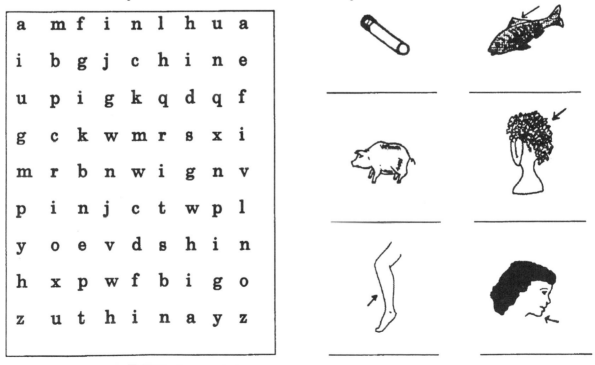

a	m	f	i	n	l	h	u	a
i	b	g	j	c	h	i	n	e
u	p	i	g	k	q	d	q	f
g	c	k	w	m	r	s	x	i
m	r	b	n	w	i	g	n	v
p	i	n	j	c	t	w	p	l
y	o	e	v	d	s	h	i	n
h	x	p	w	f	b	i	g	o
z	u	t	h	i	n	a	y	z

_____   _____

_____   _____

_____   _____

72

When Does 1 + 1 = 1 ?

LOOK !

mail   +   man   =   mailman

In the exercise below, choose a word from the box and add it to the one on the list to make a compound word.

saw   tail   pin   pack   deep   shape

1. hat _____   4. jig _____

2. pig _____   5. ship _____

3. back _____   6. chin- _____

Is an Inch Big or Little?

This is a one-inch ant.

THAT IS BIG !

This is an itsy-bitsy one-inch pig.

That is little.

If a one-inch ant is big,

And a one-inch pig is little,

Do you think an inch is big or little ?

---

*The minimum number of words expected to be read per minute is 85.
There are 49 words in this material (including title). With practice the student should be able to read it in about 33 seconds.

73

Name _____   Date _____

1. Have the pupil go over the lists of words at the top of the exercise. Point out to the pupil that the ending of each word is the same. Examples: *fill* *hill* *will*.
2. Next have the pupil do the exercise, crossing out the two words that are incorrect.
3. When all the sentences have been done in this way, the pupil returns to the first sentence and *orally* reads each sentence with the correct word.

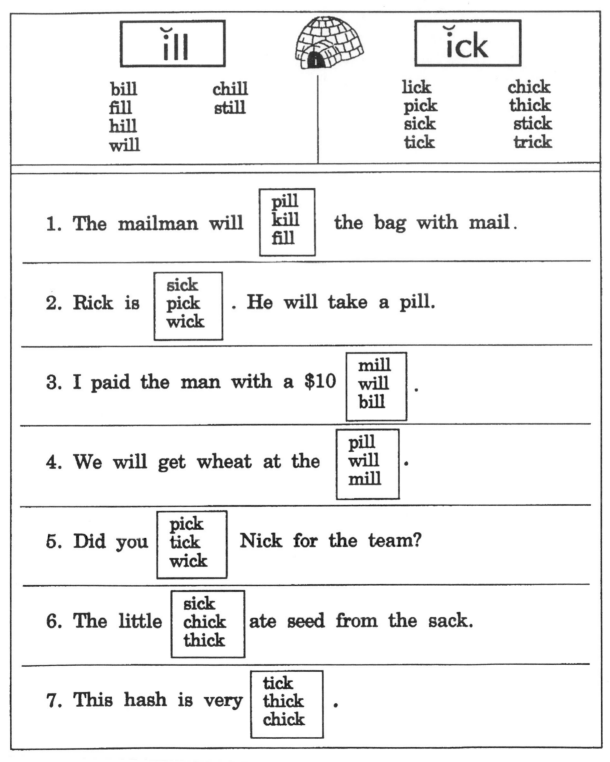

ĭll

bill   chill
fill   still
hill
will

ĭck

lick   chick
pick   thick
sick   stick
tick   trick

1. The mailman will
   pill
   kill
   fill
   the bag with mail.

2. Rick is
   sick
   pick
   wick
   . He will take a pill.

3. I paid the man with a $10
   mill
   will
   bill
   .

4. We will get wheat at the
   pill
   will
   mill
   .

5. Did you
   pick
   tick
   wick
   Nick for the team?

6. The little
   sick
   chick
   thick
   ate seed from the sack.

7. This hash is very
   tick
   thick
   chick
   .

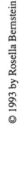

Name _____   Date _____

Trace over the word three or four times. Next, write the word in the space provided.

This side for those who print.   **This side for those who use cursive.**

ill   *ill*

fill   *fill*

hill   *hill*

will   *will*

ick   *ick*

sick   *sick*

lick   *lick*

thick   *thick*

Name _____ Date _____

In the following sentences fill in the missing letter to complete the word.

1. Jack and Jill went up the ___ ill.	m	h	b
2. Rick is sick. The [doctor] will give him a ___ ill.	s	f	p
3. I need some wheat. Will you ___ ill this sack for me?	s	b	f
4. Dad will give me a $5 ___ ill to weed the [garden].	p	f	b
5. ___ ick and I will go to the game.	P	R	K
6. This hash is too ___ ick.	th	ch	wh
7. The [dog] will ___ ick the dish.	l	t	w
8. The ___ ick said "Peep Peep".	sh	ch	th
9. Did you ___ ick the best team to win?	s	t	p
10. The ___ ick on this [candle] is out.	k	w	s

Name _____ Date _____

Read the words under each box. Draw a picture for the words.

a $10 bill

a chick

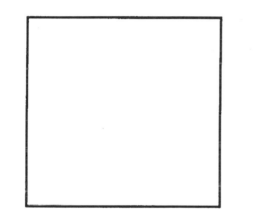

a stick

a pig

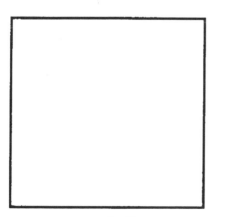

a hill

a windmill

Name _____   Date _____

1. Have the pupil go over the lists of words at the top of the exercise. Point out to the pupil that the ending of each word is the same. Examples: *fish* *dish* *wish*.
2. Next have the pupil do the exercises, crossing out the two words that are incorrect.
3. When all the sentences have been done in this way, the returns to the first sentence and *orally* reads each sentence with the correct word.

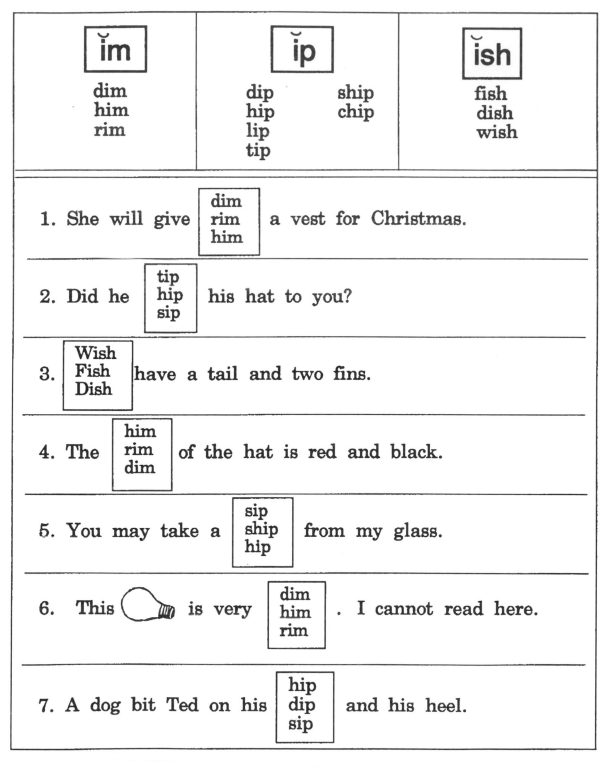

ĭm	ĭp	ĭsh
dim him rim	dip ship hip chip lip tip	fish dish wish

1. She will give | dim
rim
him | a vest for Christmas.

2. Did he | tip
hip
sip | his hat to you?

3. | Wish
Fish
Dish | have a tail and two fins.

4. The | him
rim
dim | of the hat is red and black.

5. You may take a | sip
ship
hip | from my glass.

6. This 🔦 is very | dim
him
rim | . I cannot read here.

7. A dog bit Ted on his | hip
dip
sip | and his heel.

Name _____   Date _____

Trace over the word three or four times. Next, write the word in the space provided.

This side for those who print.   This side for those who use cursive.

ish   *ish*

fish   *fish*

wish   *wish*

dish   *dish*

ip   *ip*

lip   *lip*

hip   *hip*

dip   *dip*

Name _____ Date _____

By changing the vowel *a* in each word to the vowel *i*, a new word is formed. The student writes the new word on the line opposite the printed word. When this is completed, the student reads aloud the old word and then the new word so that the difference in vowel sounds can be heard.

ă	ĭ
1. sap.............................	sip
2. bag.............................	_____
3. sack............................	_____
4. lap.............................	_____
5. hat.............................	_____
6. pan............................	_____
7. tap.............................	_____
8. sat.............................	_____
9. had............................	_____
10. wag...........................	_____
11. tack...........................	_____
12. tan............................	_____
13. dad...........................	_____
14. fan............................	_____
15. ham...........................	_____
16. fat............................	_____
17. pat............................	_____
18. pack..........................	_____
19. flap...........................	_____
20. clap..........................	_____

Name _____   Date _____

These are difficult multisyllable words at this level. However, explain to the pupil that if he/she can figure out the part that is underlined and use the context clues, it will be less difficult to decode the word. Practice helps.

1. The 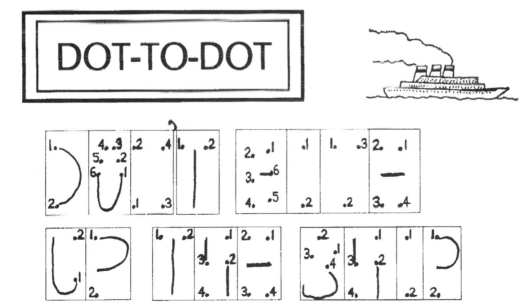 had a <u>dim</u>ple on each cheek.	dimple
2. We had fish and chips for <u>din</u>ner.	dinner
3. The <u>hip</u>popotamus is a very big animal.	hippopotamus
4. Do not wake the ⌂ . Go on <u>tip</u>toe.	tiptoe
5. The <u>dish</u>rag is in the <u>dish</u>pan.	dishrag dishpan
6. I cannot pay all that cash for this van. This is a <u>rip</u>off.	ripoff

DOT-TO-DOT

_____ _____ _____   _____ _____ _____

Name _____   Date _____

1. Explain to the pupil that all the pictures on this page begin with the same vowel sound as the word *igloo*.
2. Read the following definitions to the pupil and point to the picture:
    a. An infant is a baby.
    b. Another word for sick is ill.
    c. Italy is a country that is shaped like a boot.
    d. Flies, ants, and bees are called insects.
    e. An igloo is a round-shaped hut made of blocks of ice.
3. Next, the pupil names each picture and writes the name from the list.

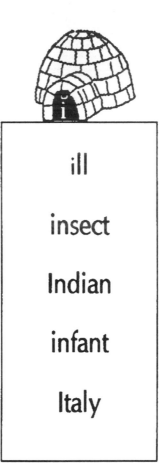

ill

insect

Indian

infant

Italy

_____

_____

_____   _____   _____

Name _____ Date _____

CHECK LIST

ĭ

big	chick	did	fig	hid
bill	chill	dig	fill	hill
bin	chin	dim	fin	him
bit	chip	dip	fit	hip
			fish	hit

jig	kill	lick	mill	pick
		lid		pig
		lip		pill
		lit		pin
				pit

rid	sick	shin	tick	wick
rim	sin	ship	till	wig
rip	sip		tin	will
Rick	sit		tip	win

Select a word and have the pupil attempt to read it. (Don't select more than a total of ten words a session.)
If the pupil is able to read the word, put a plus (+) mark in front of the word.
If the pupil is not able to read the word, put a minus (-) mark and change it into a plus when the pupil can recognize it.
Make flash cards of the unsuccessful words for practice.

83

© 1993 by Rosella Bernstein

Name _____   Date _____

1. Have the pupil go over the lists of words at the top of the exercise. Point out to the pupil that the ending of each word is the same. Examples: b*ike*   h*ike*   l*ike*.
2. Next have the pupil do the exercise, crossing out the two words that are incorrect.
3. When all the sentences have been done in this way, the pupil returns to the first sentence and *orally* reads each sentence with the correct word.

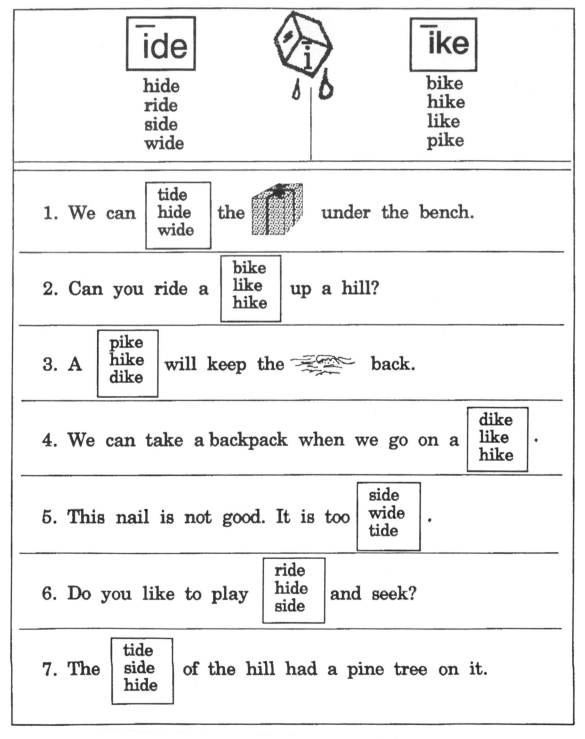

īde	**īke**
hide	bike
ride	hike
side	like
wide	pike

1. We can [tide / hide / wide] the ▨ under the bench.

2. Can you ride a [bike / like / hike] up a hill?

3. A [pike / hike / dike] will keep the 〰 back.

4. We can take a backpack when we go on a [dike / like / hike] .

5. This nail is not good. It is too [side / wide / tide] .

6. Do you like to play [ride / hide / side] and seek?

7. The [tide / side / hide] of the hill had a pine tree on it.

84

Trace over the word three or four times. Next write the word in the space provided.

This side for those who print.   This side for those who use cursive.

ide   *ide*

hide   *hide*

ride   *ride*

side   *side*

ike   *ike*

bike   *bike*

like   *like*

hike   *hike*

Name _____   Date _____

Answer the question with one or more words. It does not have to be a complete sentence.

1. I have a black and red bike.

   You have a black and red bike.

   What do we have?

   _____

2. Dan will take a hike in the rain.

   Ted will take a hike in the rain.

   What will Ted and Dan do?

   _____

3. Pam cannot dig for clams when the tide is in.

   She can dig for clams when the tide is out.

   When can Pam dig for clams?

   _____

4. Jean will sit by my side.

   Sam will not sit by my side.

   Who will sit by my side?

   _____

5. Jack will take a ride by the lake.

   Jake will take a ride by the dam.

   Who will take a ride by the dam?

   _____

© 1993 by Rosella Bernstein

Name _____   Date _____

I. Choose a rhyming word that makes sense and write it in the blank.

---

1. I like to ride

   With you by my _____ .   tide   side   wide

---

2. Mike ran over a spike

   With his new yellow_____ . pike   bike   hike

---

3. I will take a hike

   I will not take my _____ . like   pike   bike

---

4. I went for a ride

   Down the _____ .   wide   slide   hide

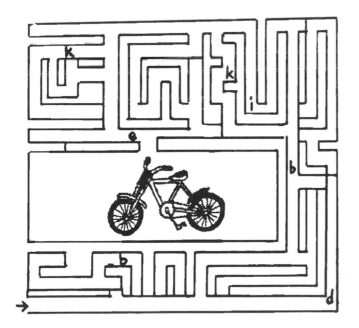

II.

A-MAZE-ING

___ ___ ___ ___ ___

Name _____   Date _____

1. Have the pupil go over the lists of words at the top of the exercise. Point out to the pupil that the ending of each word is the same. Examples: *fight   night   light*.
2. Next have the pupil do the exercise, crossing out the two words that are incorrect.
3. When all the sentences have been done in this way, the pupil returns to the first sentence and *orally* reads each sentence with the correct word.

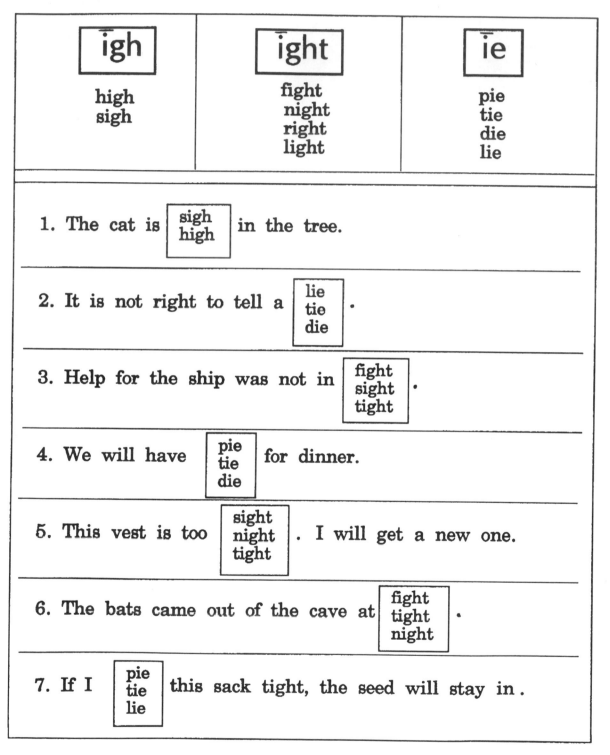

igh	ight	ie
high sigh	fight night right light	pie tie die lie

1. The cat is [sigh / high] in the tree.

2. It is not right to tell a [lie / tie / die] .

3. Help for the ship was not in [fight / sight / tight] .

4. We will have [pie / tie / die] for dinner.

5. This vest is too [sight / night / tight] . I will get a new one.

6. The bats came out of the cave at [fight / tight / night] .

7. If I [pie / tie / lie] this sack tight, the seed will stay in .

Name _____   Date _____

Trace over the word three or four times. Next, write the word in the space provided.

This side for those who print.   This side for those who use cursive.

ie   *ie*

tie   *tie*

pie   *pie*

lie   *lie*

ight   *ight*

night   *night*

right   *right*

fight   *fight*

Name _____ Date _____

Write the name of the picture in the blank.
Look for the word in the puzzle and draw a line around it.

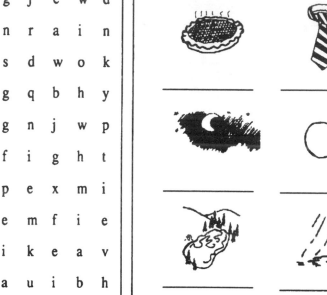

a	b	y	v	r	i	g	h	t	f	q	a
r	o	h	l	a	k	e	g	j	c	w	d
p	i	e	n	y	f	n	n	r	a	i	n
m	t	e	u	u	t	e	s	d	w	o	k
h	o	l	i	g	h	t	g	q	b	h	y
n	e	l	s	o	a	k	g	n	j	w	p
i	v	e	n	h	g	l	f	i	g	h	t
g	g	t	c	b	r	y	p	e	x	m	i
h	i	y	z	t	k	w	e	m	f	i	e
t	j	c	d	q	p	b	i	k	e	a	v
z	l	y	a	s	j	o	a	u	i	b	h

!!

Bright Sayings

1. The fat is in the fire.

2. Out of sight, out of mind.

3. When the cat's away the mice will play.

4. You made your bed, now lie in it.

5. A cat has nine lives.

6. Right makes might.

Name _____   Date _____

I.

When does 1 + 1 = 1 ?

high + way = highway

1. hay + _____ = _____

2. tie + _____ = _____

3. hitch+ _____ = _____

4. flash+ _____ = _____

Choose a word from this list to make a compound word.

light

pin

ride

hike

II.

ACROSS →

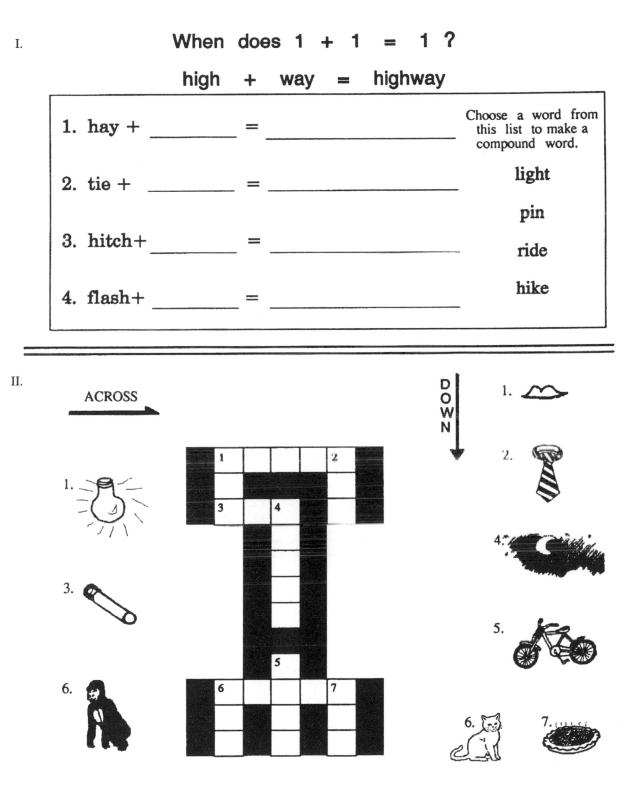

DOWN ↓

91

Name _____   Date _____

1. Have the pupil go over the lists of words at the top of the exercise. Point out to the pupil that the ending of each
   word is the same. Examples: m*ice*   n*ice*   r*ice*.
2. Next have the pupil do the exercise, crossing out the two words that are incorrect.
3. When all the sentences have been done in this way, the pupil returns to the first sentence and *orally* reads each
   sentence with the correct word.

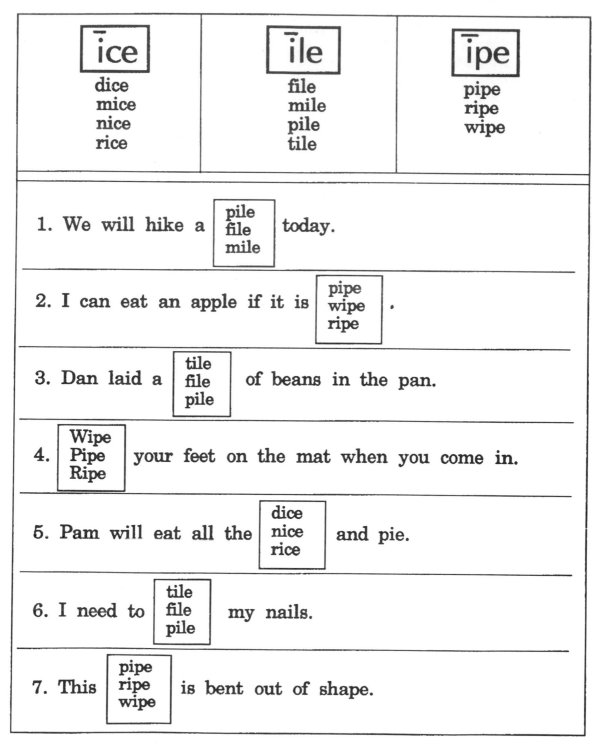

¯ice	¯ile	¯ipe
dice	file	pipe
mice	mile	ripe
nice	pile	wipe
rice	tile	

1. We will hike a [pile / file / mile] today.

2. I can eat an apple if it is [pipe / wipe / ripe] .

3. Dan laid a [tile / file / pile] of beans in the pan.

4. [Wipe / Pipe / Ripe] your feet on the mat when you come in.

5. Pam will eat all the [dice / nice / rice] and pie.

6. I need to [tile / file / pile] my nails.

7. This [pipe / ripe / wipe] is bent out of shape.

Name _____   Date _____

Trace over the word three or four times. Next, write the word in the space provided.

This side for those who print.   This side for those who use cursive.

ile   *ile*

mile   *mile*

pile   *pile*

file   *file*

ice   *ice*

nice   *nice*

mice   *mice*

rice   *rice*

Name _____ Date _____

I. Unscramble the following words. Tell the pupil that these are long *i* words and that they end in a silent *e*.

e p p i   e f i l   c r e i

_____   _____   _____

e i m c   p i r e   e c i l

_____   _____   _____

w p i e   l m e i   i e n c

_____   _____   _____

II. The pupil reads the word at the beginning of the sentence and decides what words should be added to make a complete sentence. If the pupil is unable to write the words, the instructor prints them. When the exercise has been completed, the pupil reads all the sentences.

1. The mice _____

2. Pile the _____

3. Wipe the _____

4. A nice _____

5. A bag of rice _____

6. I will file _____

7. I ate a ripe _____

8. We need the pipe for _____

9. A mile from here _____

10. The tile _____

nice	bike	hide	night	sick
bid	dig	tie	ripe	dish
ride	lip		hike	fight
dim	file	fish	bill	pin
lie	rice	mile	wipe	bright

I. Mark each word with a long or short mark. Long *i* BINGO can be either across, down, or diagonal.

II. Write the proper vowel or vowels in the blank in the following exercise.

1. p__pe		9. m __ ce	
2. w__ ve		10. d __ ce	
3. p __ n		11. p__e	
4. n __ t		12. t__e	
5. j__ __p		13. n__ ght	
6. b__ckp__ck		14. sh__ __p	
7. g__me		15. r__ __ n	
8. b__ __k		16. r__ y	

Name _____ Date _____

1. Have the pupil go over the lists of words at the top of the exercise. Point out to the pupil that the ending of each word is the same. Examples: *fine*   *nine*   sh*ine*.
2. Next have the pupil do the exercise, crossing out the two words that are incorrect.
3. When all the sentences have been done in this way, the pupil returns to the first sentence and *orally* reads each sentence with the correct word.

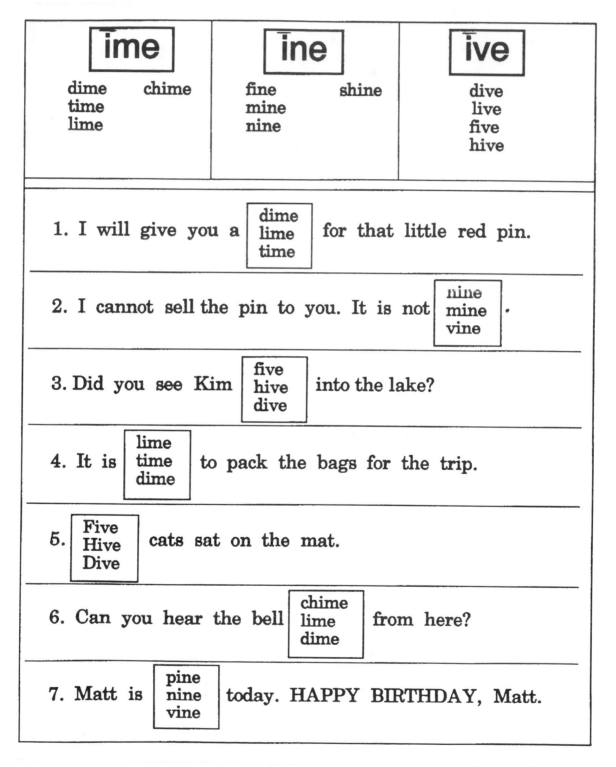

īme	īne	īve
dime chime time lime	fine shine mine nine	dive live five hive

1. I will give you a ⎡dime⎤ ⎢lime⎥ ⎣time⎦ for that little red pin.

2. I cannot sell the pin to you. It is not ⎡nine⎤ ⎢mine⎥ ⎣vine⎦ .

3. Did you see Kim ⎡five⎤ ⎢hive⎥ ⎣dive⎦ into the lake?

4. It is ⎡lime⎤ ⎢time⎥ ⎣dime⎦ to pack the bags for the trip.

5. ⎡Five⎤ ⎢Hive⎥ ⎣Dive⎦ cats sat on the mat.

6. Can you hear the bell ⎡chime⎤ ⎢lime⎥ ⎣dime⎦ from here?

7. Matt is ⎡pine⎤ ⎢nine⎥ ⎣vine⎦ today. HAPPY BIRTHDAY, Matt.

Name _____   Date _____

Trace over the word three or four times. Next, write the word in the space provided.

This side for those who print.   This side for those who use cursive.

ine   *ine*

mine   *mine*

line   *line*

nine   *nine*

ive   *ive*

five   *five*

hive   *hive*

dive   *dive*

Name _____   Date _____

I. The student copies the word on the blank line and adds the letter *e*. When this is completed, the student reads aloud the old word and then the new word so that the difference in vowel sounds can be heard.

ĭ   ī

1. bit   1. ___bite_____

2. dim   2. _____

3. fin   3. _____

4. hid   4. _____

5. kit   5. _____

6. pin   6. _____

7. rid   7. _____

8. rip   8. _____

9. shin   9. _____

10. slim   10. _____

II.

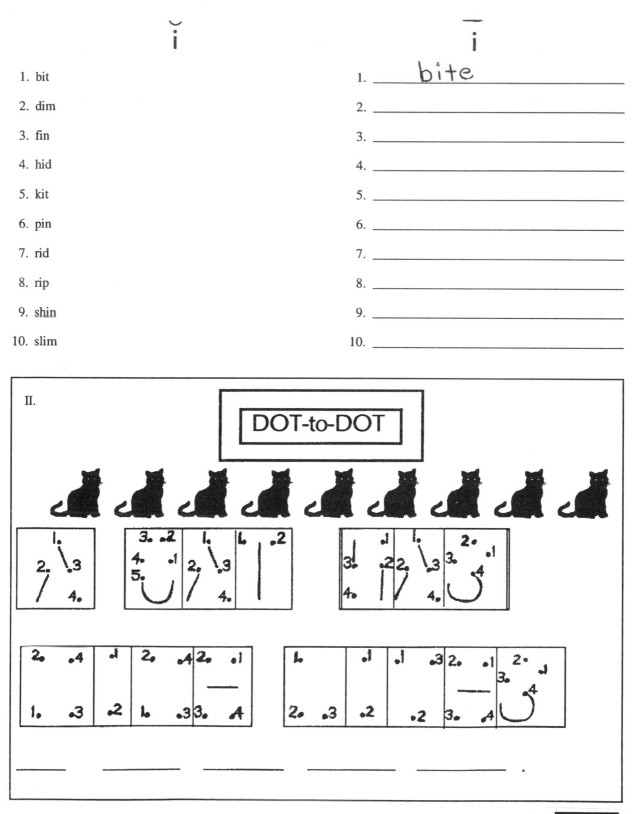

DOT-to-DOT

___ ___   ___ ___   ___ ___ ___ .

98

Name _____ Date _____

CHECK LIST

$\overline{\text{i}}$

bike	chime	dike	fight	hide
		die	file	hike
		dice	fine	hive
		dime	five	
		dine		
		dive		

like	might	night	side	shine
light	mice	nice	sight	
lie	mile			
lice	mine			
lime				
line				
live				

tide	vine	wide
tight		wipe
tie		
tile		
time		

Select a word and have the pupil attempt to read it. (Don't select more than a total of ten words at a session.)
If the pupil is able to read the word, put a plus (+) mark in front of the word.
If he/she is not able to read the word, put a minus (-) mark and make flash cards of the unsuccessful words for practice.

Name _____ Date _____

1. Have the pupil go over the lists of words at the top of the exercise. Point out to the pupil that the ending of each word is the same. Examples: *rock* *lock* *clock*.
2. Next have the pupil do the exercise, crossing out the two words that are incorrect.
3. When all the sentences have been done in this way, the pupil returns to the first sentence and *orally* reads each sentence with the correct word.

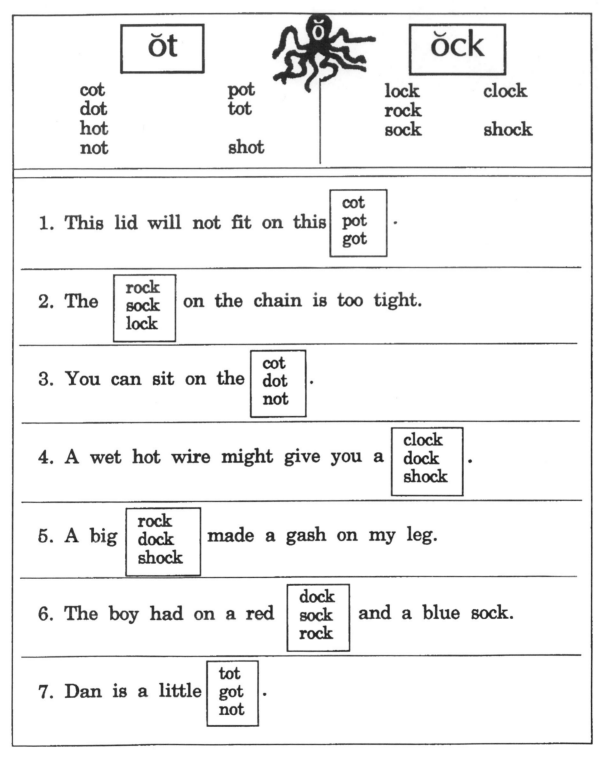

ŏt		ŏck	
cot	pot	lock	clock
dot	tot	rock	
hot		sock	shock
not	shot		

1. This lid will not fit on this [cot / pot / got] .

2. The [rock / sock / lock] on the chain is too tight.

3. You can sit on the [cot / dot / not] .

4. A wet hot wire might give you a [clock / dock / shock] .

5. A big [rock / dock / shock] made a gash on my leg.

6. The boy had on a red [dock / sock / rock] and a blue sock.

7. Dan is a little [tot / got / not] .

Name _____   Date _____

Trace over the word three or four times. Next, write the word in the space provided.

This side for those who print.   This side for those who use cursive.

ot   _ot_

hot   _hot_

got   _got_

dot   _dot_

ock   _ock_

rock   _rock_

sock   _sock_

lock   _lock_

© 1953 by Rosella Bernstein

I. Read the two words at the right of each sentence. Then write the word in the blank that makes sense. When the exercise is completed, the pupil orally reads every sentence.

1. The ship was at the _____ .   dock   sock

2. I cannot pick up this pan.

   It is too _____ .   cot   hot

3. The hot wire gave Ted a _____.   lock   shock

4. We _____ a lot of maps for the trip.   pot   got

5. The _____ fell off the cliff.   dock   rock

6. A red _____ of paint got on his new bike.   dot   hot

II. Mark the short vowel words like this: pǎn

Mark the long vowel words like this: pāin

1. sock	6. peck	11. maid
2. mash	7. lock	12. shock
3. tame	8. mean	13. dot
4. pot	9. time	14. right
5. team	10. not	15. west

Name _____   Date _____

I. Put a line around the picture that rhymes with the word on the left.

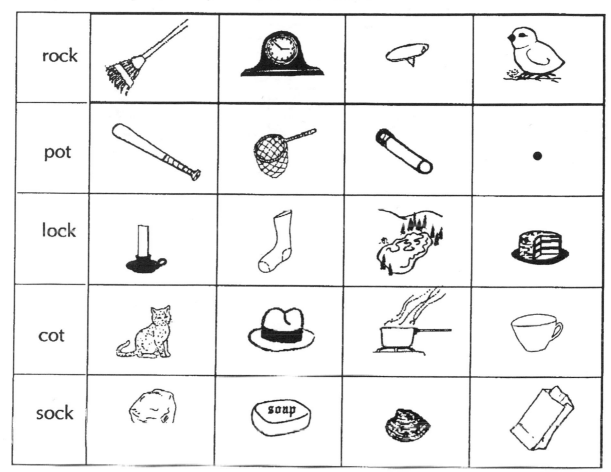

rock				
pot				
lock				
cot				
sock				

II.

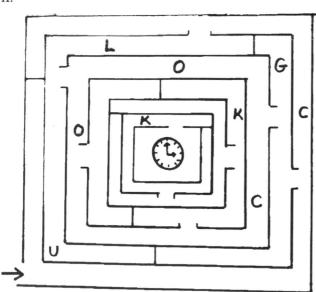

A-MAZE-ING

_ _ _ _ _ _ _ _

Name _____   Date _____

1. Have the pupil go over the lists of words at the top of the exercise. Point out to the pupil that the ending of each word is the same. Examples: m*op*   h*op*   sh*op*.
2. Next have the pupil do the exercise, crossing out the two words that are incorrect.
3. When all the sentences have been done in this way, the pupil returns to the first sentence and *orally* reads each sentence with the correct word.

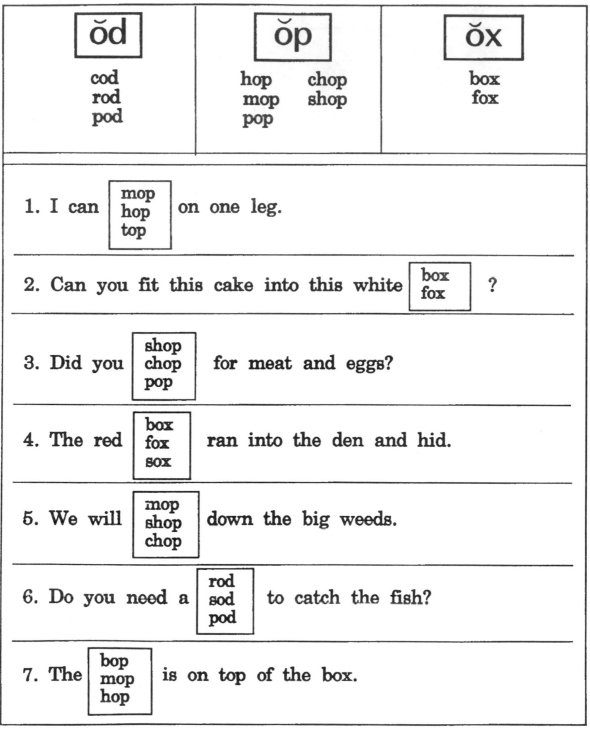

ŏd	ŏp	ŏx
cod	hop chop	box
rod	mop shop	fox
pod	pop	

1. I can | mop / hop / top | on one leg.

2. Can you fit this cake into this white | box / fox | ?

3. Did you | shop / chop / pop | for meat and eggs?

4. The red | box / fox / sox | ran into the den and hid.

5. We will | mop / shop / chop | down the big weeds.

6. Do you need a | rod / sod / pod | to catch the fish?

7. The | bop / mop / hop | is on top of the box.

Trace over the word three or four times. Next write the word in the space provided.

This side for those who print.   This side for those who use cursive.

op   op

hop   hop

mop   mop

pop   pop

ox   ox

fox   fox

box   box

sox   sox

Name _____ Date _____

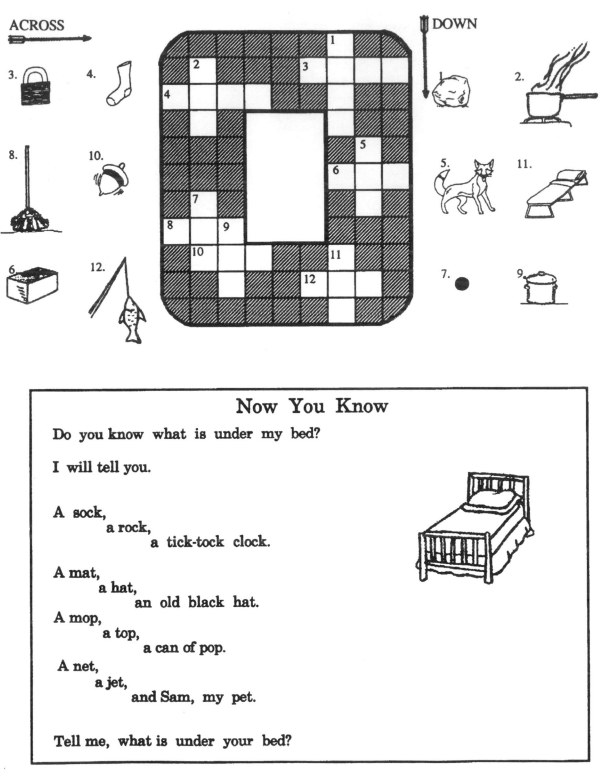

ACROSS

3. 4. 8. 10. 6. 12.

DOWN

2. 5. 11. 7. 9.

Now You Know

Do you know what is under my bed?

I will tell you.

A sock,
    a rock,
        a tick-tock clock.

A mat,
    a hat,
        an old black hat.

A mop,
    a top,
        a can of pop.

A net,
    a jet,
        and Sam, my pet.

Tell me, what is under your bed?

There are 54 words in this poem, including the title. With practice the pupil should be able to read it in approximately 34 seconds.

Name _____ Date _____

These are difficult multisyllable words at this level. However, explain to the pupil that if he/she can figure out the part that is underlined and use the context clues, it will be less difficult to decode the word. Practice helps.

1. I have a dime in my <u>pock</u>et.   pocket

2. This pot is made of <u>copp</u>er and steel.   copper

3. The <u>box</u>er fell on the mat and did not get up.   boxer

4. The 🐓 said, "<u>Cock</u>-a-doodle-doo."   Cock

5. The <u>rock</u>et went up like a beam of light.   rocket

6. When I go to the beach I like to get a <u>pop</u>sicle.   popsicle

7. Hickory, Dickory, <u>Dock</u>.   Dock

   The 🐭 ran up the clock.

In the exercise below, put a line around the words that goes with the picture.

A fox on a box A fox on a bed	
A fish on a rock A fish on a rod	
A man and a mop A man and a map	
An ax that can shop An ax that can chop	

Name _____   Date _____

1. Have the pupil go over the lists of words at the top of the exercise. Point out to the pupil that the ending of each word is the same. Examples: d*og*   f*og*   fr*og*.
2. Next have the pupil do the exercise, crossing out the two words that are incorrect.
3. When all the sentences have been done in this way, the pupil returns to the first sentence and *orally* reads each sentence with the correct word.

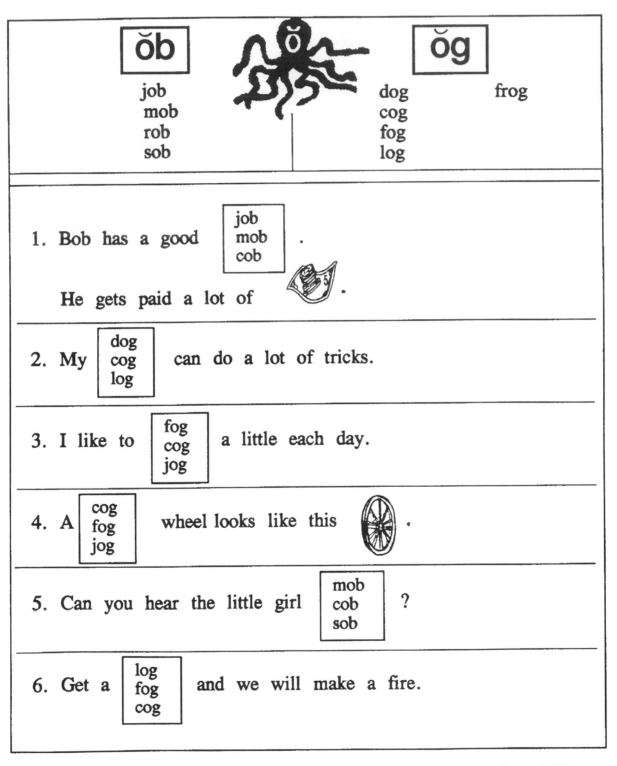

ŏb		ŏg	
job		dog	frog
mob		cog	
rob		fog	
sob		log	

1. Bob has a good
   - job
   - mob
   - cob
   .

   He gets paid a lot of _____ .

2. My
   - dog
   - cog
   - log
   can do a lot of tricks.

3. I like to
   - fog
   - cog
   - jog
   a little each day.

4. A
   - cog
   - fog
   - jog
   wheel looks like this _____ .

5. Can you hear the little girl
   - mob
   - cob
   - sob
   ?

6. Get a
   - log
   - fog
   - cog
   and we will make a fire.

Name _____   Date _____

Trace over the word three or four times. Next, write the word in the space provided.

This side for those who print.   This side for those who use cursive.

ob   ob

job   job

cob   cob

Bob   Bob

og   og

dog   dog

fog   fog

log   log

Name _____ Date _____

Put an X in front of the word that names the picture.

_____ bonnet

_____ bottle

_____ rocket

_____ robin

_____ dominoes

_____ dollhouse

_____ popcorn

_____ pocket

_____ topping

_____ toggle

_____ lobster

_____ lockjaw

_____ lobby

_____ locket

_____ popsicle

_____ possum

Name _____   Date _____

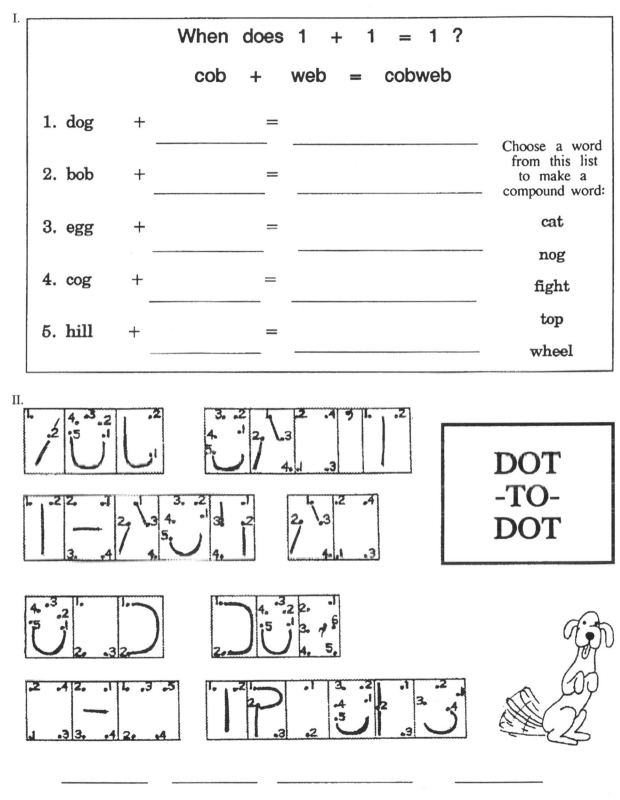

I.

When does 1 + 1 = 1 ?

cob + web = cobweb

1. dog + _____ = _____
2. bob + _____ = _____
3. egg + _____ = _____
4. cog + _____ = _____
5. hill + _____ = _____

Choose a word from this list to make a compound word:

cat

nog

fight

top

wheel

II.

DOT -TO- DOT

_____ _____ _____ _____

_____ _____ _____

111

Name _____ Date _____

1. Explain to the pupil that all the pictures on this page begin with the same vowel sound as the word *octopus*.
2. Read the following definitions to the pupil as you point to the picture:
   a. *Oxen* are work animals.
   b. 1, 3, 5, 7, and 9 are *odd,* numbers.
      2, 4, 6, 8, and 10 are even numbers.
   c. An *otter* has short, thick, glossy fur like a seal.
      It has short legs and a thick tail.
      It is a good swimmer.
   d. An *octagon* is a figure that has eight sides.
3. Next, the pupil names each picture and writes the name from the list.

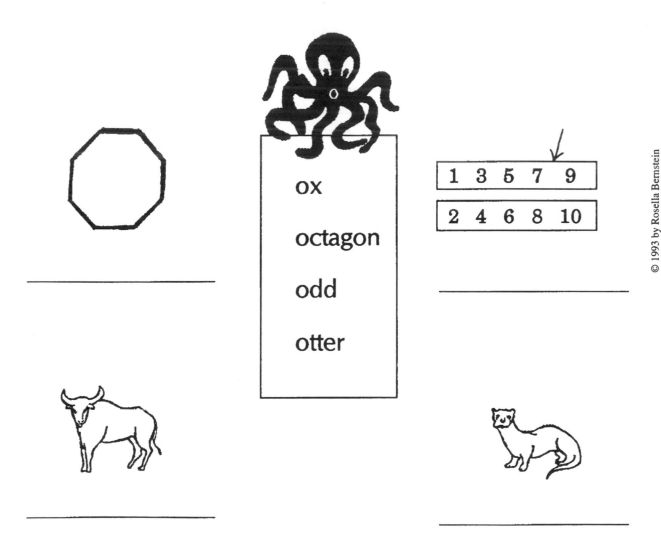

ox

octagon

odd

otter

1 3 5 7 9

2 4 6 8 10

_____

_____

_____

_____

CHECK LIST

$$\breve{o}$$

Bob	cob	chop	dot	fog
bop	cod		dock	fox
box	cog			
	cop			
	cot			
	cock			

God	hop	job	log	mop
got	hot	jog	lot	mob
	hog	jot	lock	

pop	rod	sob	shock	top
pot	rob	sod	shop	tot
pod	rot	sock	shot	
	rock			

Select a word and have the pupil attempt to read it. (Don't select more than a total of ten words a session.)
If the pupil is able to read the word, put a plus (+) mark in front of the word.
If the pupil is not able to read the word, put a minus (-) mark and change it into a plus when the pupil can recognize it.
Make flash cards of the unsuccessful words for practice.

1. Have the pupil go over the lists of words at the top of the exercise. Point out to the pupil that the ending of each word is the same. Examples: **bone** **cone** **tone**.
2. Next have the pupil do the exercise, crossing out the two words that are incorrect.
3. When all the sentences have been done in this way, the pupil returns to the first sentence and *orally* reads each sentence with the correct word.

ōke	**ōle**	**ōne**
joke	hole	bone
poke	pole	cone
woke	mole	tone

1. I have a _____ in my sock.

          pole
          hole
          mole

2. Do not _____ the cat with a rake.

          poke
          woke
          joke

3. At the _____ the time will be one P.M.

          bone
          cone
          tone

4. The flag is high on the _____.

          pole
          mole
          hole

5. I will tell you a funny _____.

          poke
          joke
          woke

6. I ate an ice cream _____ for lunch.

          bone
          tone
          cone

7. Dad _____ us at five A.M. to go fishing.

          woke
          joke
          poke

Name _____   Date _____

1. Have the pupil go over the lists of words at the top of the exercise. Point out to the pupil that the ending of each word is the same. Examples: **bone**   **cone**   **tone**.
2. Next have the pupil do the exercise, crossing out the two words that are incorrect.
3. When all the sentences have been done in this way, the pupil returns to the first sentence and *orally* reads each sentence with the correct word.

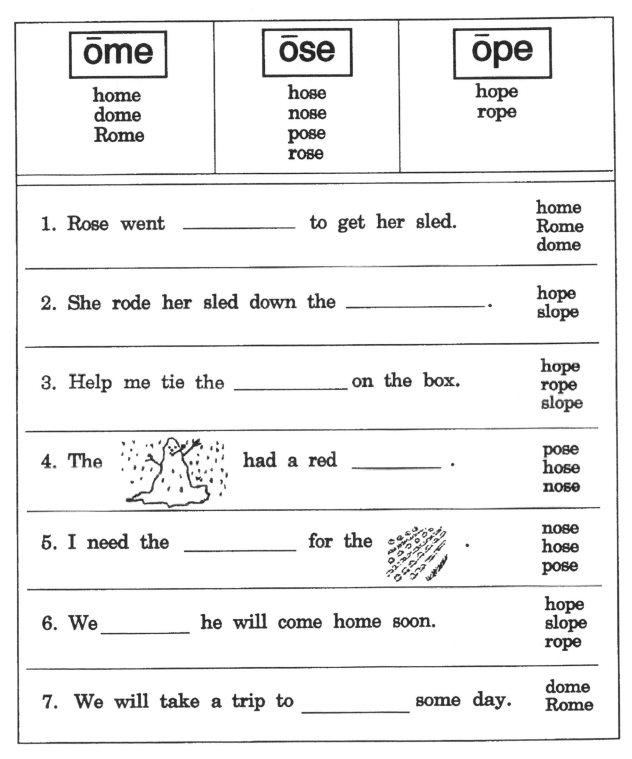

ōme	ōse	ōpe
home	hose	hope
dome	nose	rope
Rome	pose	
	rose	

1. Rose went _____ to get her sled.
   home
   Rome
   dome

2. She rode her sled down the _____ .
   hope
   slope

3. Help me tie the _____ on the box.
   hope
   rope
   slope

4. The [snowman] had a red _____ .
   pose
   hose
   ~~nose~~

5. I need the _____ for the [grass] .
   nose
   hose
   pose

6. We _____ he will come home soon.
   hope
   slope
   rope

7. We will take a trip to _____ some day.
   dome
   Rome

Trace over the word three or four times. Next, write the word in the space provided.

This side for those who print.   This side for those who use cursive.

oke   *oke*

joke   *joke*

poke   *poke*

woke   *woke*

ose   *ose*

rose   *rose*

nose   *nose*

hose   *hose*

Name _____ Date _____

I.

woke   hope   more   cone   wore

sore   role   pole   joke   poke

tore   nose   rose   tone   bone

$\bar{o}$	koej _____	omre _____	obne _____
rote _____	lope _____	onte _____	kweo _____
lore _____	ehpo _____	ower _____	kope _____
oser _____	oser _____	enco _____	esno _____

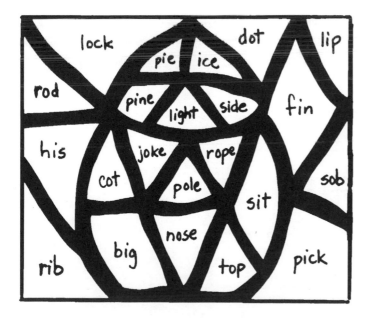

PICTURE SHOW

___ ___ ___ ___ ___

II. Color pink all the sections that have long *i* words. Color brown all the sections that have long *o* words. Do not color any other sections.

Change the Vowel
Make a New Word

$\overline{i}$	to	$\overline{o}$
dime	⟶	_dome_
line	⟶	
mile	⟶	
pike	⟶	
ripe	⟶	
ride	⟶	

$\overline{a}$	to	$\overline{o}$
cane	⟶	
pale	⟶	
Jake	⟶	
lane	⟶	
male	⟶	
wake	⟶	

After the pupil is finished writing all the new words, the original word is read aloud and then the new word is read aloud. Example: dime   dome.

Name _____   Date _____

1. Have the pupil go over the lists of words at the top of the exercise. Point out to the pupil that the ending of each word is the same. Examples: *goat*   *boat*   *coat*.
2. Next have the pupil do the exercise, crossing out the two words that are incorrect.
3. When all the sentences have been done in this way, the pupil returns to the first sentence and *orally* reads each sentence with the correct word.

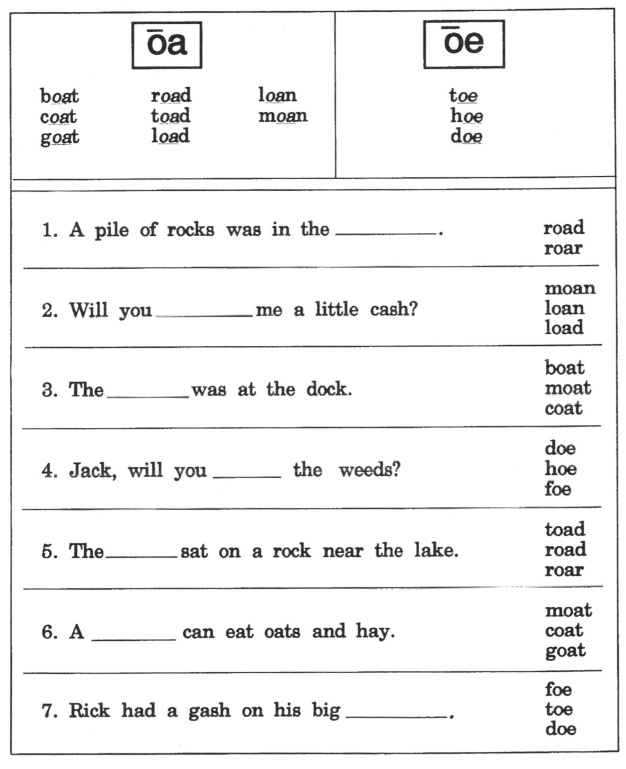

$\overline{\text{o}}$a			$\overline{\text{o}}$e
boat	road	loan	toe
coat	toad	moan	hoe
goat	load		doe

1. A pile of rocks was in the _____.   road
                                              roar

2. Will you _____ me a little cash?   moan
                                              loan
                                              load

3. The _____ was at the dock.   boat
                                              moat
                                              coat

4. Jack, will you _____ the weeds?   doe
                                              hoe
                                              foe

5. The _____ sat on a rock near the lake. toad
                                              road
                                              roar

6. A _____ can eat oats and hay.   moat
                                              coat
                                              goat

7. Rick had a gash on his big _____.   foe
                                              toe
                                              doe

119

Name _____   Date _____

Trace over the word three or four times. Next, write the word in the space provided.

This side for those who print.   This side for those who use cursive.

oat   *oat*

boat   *boat*

coat   *coat*

goat   *goat*

oe   *oe*

toe   *toe*

hoe   *hoe*

Joe   *Joe*

Name _____   Date _____

road
read
toast
toad   boat
        bait
toe   cot
tie   coat
hay
hoe
doe   sop
day   soap

I. Draw a line around the word that goes
    with one of the pictures on the right.
    Write the word under the picture.

II.

Things That Go Together

bone	feet	coat	slippers	pole
stem	weed	face	hop	ice cream

1. toes and _____

2. hat and _____

3. dog and _____

4. robe and _____

5. hoe and _____

6. cone and _____

7. nose and _____

8. flag and _____

9. rose and _____

10. toad and _____

121

Read the first two sentences in each section. Write the word in the blank in the third sentence.

A. He saw the toad in the road.

She saw the toad in the road.

They saw the _____ in the road.

B. He will paint the van.

She will paint the boat.

She will paint the boat and he will paint the _____ .

C. The blue coat is tight on me.

The red coat is tight on me.

Each _____ is tight on me.

D. I saw a dog.

I saw a doe.

I saw a dog and a _____ .

E. A rake is in the box.

A hoe is in the box.

A rake and a _____ are in the box.

F. He has soap on his big right toe.

He has soap on his big left toe.

He has soap on each big _____ .

G. A goat likes oats.

A dog likes bones.

A dog likes bones and a goat likes _____ .

Name _____ Date _____

1. Have the pupil go over the lists of words at the top of the exercise. Point out to the pupil that the ending of each word is the same. Examples: b*ow*   m*ow*   sl*ow*.
2. Next have the pupil do the exercise, crossing out the two words that are incorrect.
3. When all the sentences have been done in this way, the pupil returns to the first sentence and *orally* reads each sentence with the correct word.

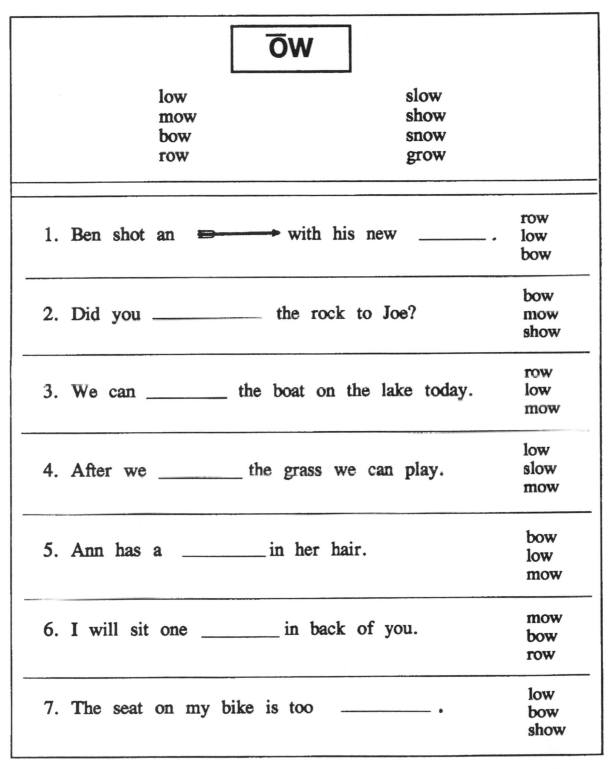

ŌW

low   slow
mow   show
bow   snow
row   grow

1. Ben shot an ➛ with his new _____ .
   row
   low
   bow

2. Did you _____ the rock to Joe?
   bow
   mow
   show

3. We can _____ the boat on the lake today.
   row
   low
   mow

4. After we _____ the grass we can play.
   low
   slow
   mow

5. Ann has a _____ in her hair.
   bow
   low
   mow

6. I will sit one _____ in back of you.
   mow
   bow
   row

7. The seat on my bike is too _____ .
   low
   bow
   show

Name _____   Date _____

Trace over the word three or four times. Next write the word in the space provided.

This side for those who print.   This side for those who use cursive.

ow   *ow*

mow   *mow*

row   *row*

bow   *bow*

glow   *glow*

snow   *snow*

show   *show*

blow   *blow*

I. Write the word that makes the most sense in the blank.

1. Yesterday we went to see a very funny _____ .

show
slow

2. We sat in the last _____ .

low
row

3. Pam wore a pretty _____ in her hair.

blow
bow

4. After the show, we went home to _____ the grass.

mow
row

5. I am glad we do not have ice and _____ yet.

snow
slow

6. We can go down to the lake to _____ our boat.

grow
row

7. The oar might hit a rock if the ~~~~ is too _____ .

low
glow

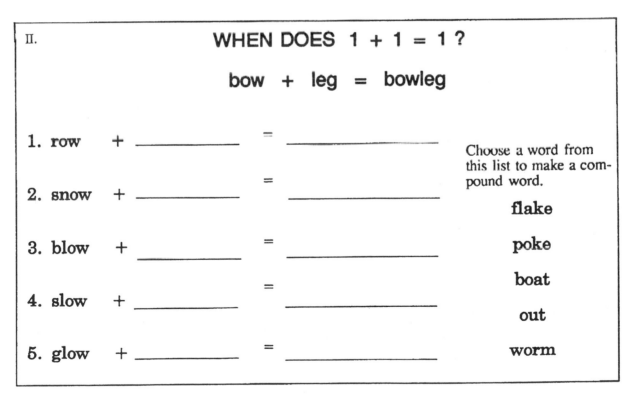

II.   WHEN DOES 1 + 1 = 1 ?

bow + leg = bowleg

1. row   + _____ = _____

2. snow + _____ = _____

3. blow + _____ = _____

4. slow + _____ = _____

5. glow + _____ = _____

Choose a word from this list to make a compound word.

flake

poke

boat

out

worm

more	rock	poke	bone	hole
shop	row	toe	rod	cob
coat	dog	ō	fox	show
clock	dot	mow	hose	fog
hoe	box	soap	frog	cot

I. Mark each word to show if it is a long o or short o. BINGO is either across, down, or diagonal. Write the BINGO words on the lines below.

_____

_____

_____

_____

_____

II.

DOT-TO-DOT

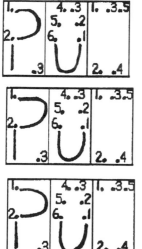

_____

CHECK LIST

$\overline{O}$

bone	cone	doe	goat	hose
boat	coat	dose		hope
bow		doze		hoe

joke	load	more	nose	poke
	loan	mole		pole
	low	moan		
		moat		
		mow		

role	sore	show	tore	wore
rose			tone	woke
rope			toad	
road			toe	
row				

Select a word and have the pupil attempt to read it. (Don't select more than a total of ten words a session.)
If the pupil is able to read the word, put a plus (+) mark in front of the word.
If the pupil is not able to read the word, put a minus (-) mark and change it into a plus when the pupil can recognize it.
Make flash cards of the unsuccessful words for practice.

Name _____   Date _____

1. Have the pupil go over the lists of words at the top of the exercise. Point out to the pupil that the ending of each word is the same. Examples: l*unch* b*unch*   p*unch*.
2. Next have the pupil do the exercise, crossing out the two words that are incorrect.
3. When all the sentences have been done in this way, the pupil returns to the first sentence and *orally* reads each sentence with the correct word.

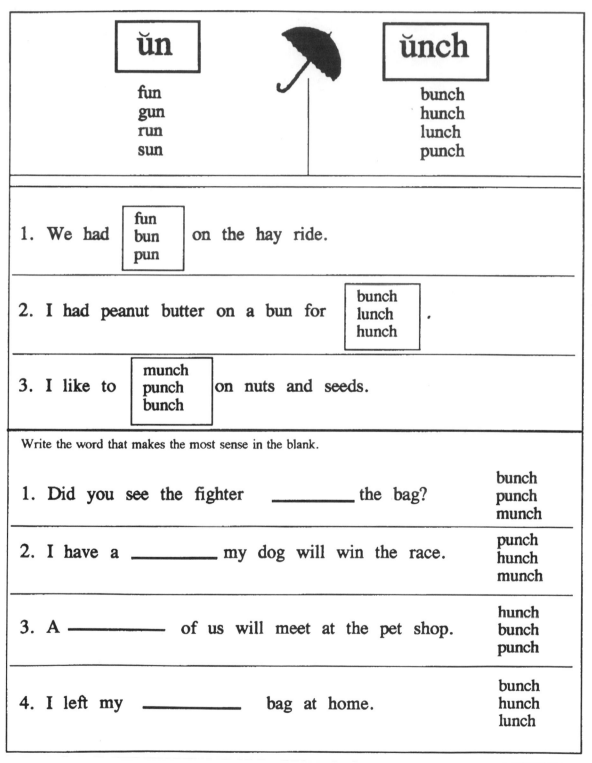

ŭn		ŭnch
fun		bunch
gun		hunch
run		lunch
sun		punch

1. We had ┌ fun / bun / pun ┐ on the hay ride.

2. I had peanut butter on a bun for ┌ bunch / lunch / hunch ┐ .

3. I like to ┌ munch / punch / bunch ┐ on nuts and seeds.

Write the word that makes the most sense in the blank.

1. Did you see the fighter _____ the bag?
bunch
punch
munch

2. I have a _____ my dog will win the race.
punch
hunch
munch

3. A _____ of us will meet at the pet shop.
hunch
bunch
punch

4. I left my _____ bag at home.
bunch
hunch
lunch

Name _____ Date _____

Trace over the word three or four times. Next, write the word in the space provided.

This side for those who print.   This side for those who use cursive.

un   *un*

fun   *fun*

run   *run*

sun   *sun*

unch   *unch*

bunch   *bunch*

lunch   *lunch*

munch   *munch*

These are difficult multisyllable words at this level. However, explain to the pupil that if he/she can figure out the part that is underlined and use the context clues, it will be less difficult to decode the word. Practice helps.

1. The bells will chime on <u>Sun</u>day.   Sunday

2. I have a <u>bun</u>dle of rags to help us clean.   bundle

3. Sam is a good <u>run</u>ner.   runner

4. <u>Sun</u>set is a nice time of day.   sunset

5. We saw a <u>fun</u>nel of smoke near the ash pile.   funnel

6. Smoke came from the <u>gun</u>shot.   gunshot

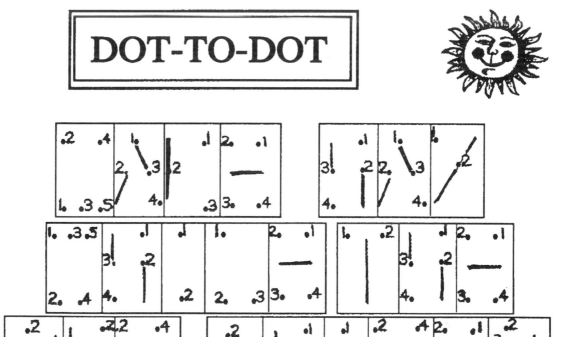

DOT-TO-DOT

___ ___ ___ ___ ___ ___ ___

Name _____   Date _____

1. Have the pupil go over the lists of words at the top of the exercise. Point out to the pupil that the ending of each word is the same. Examples: *gum* *hum* *sum*.
2. Next have the pupil do the exercise, crossing out the two words that are incorrect.
3. When all the sentences have been done in this way, the pupil returns to the first sentence and *orally* reads each sentence with the correct word.

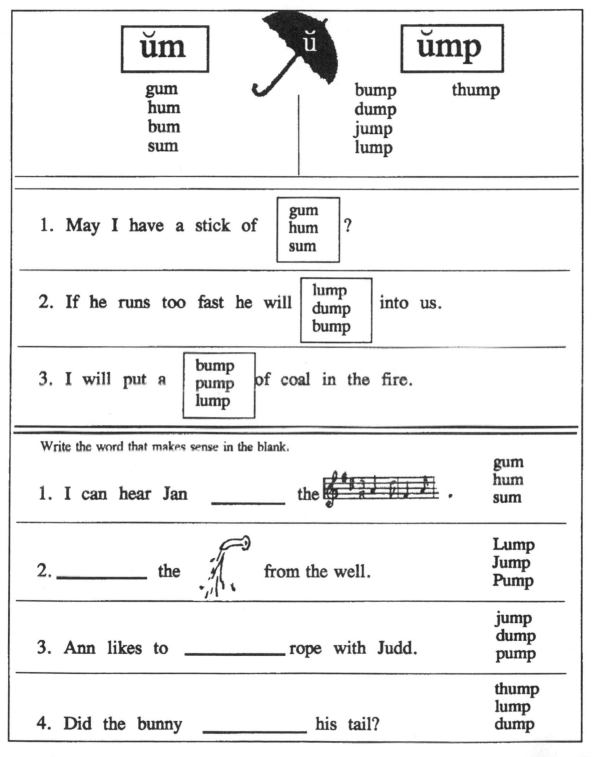

ŭm   ŭ   **ŭmp**

gum   bump   thump
hum   dump
bum   jump
sum   lump

1. May I have a stick of | gum / hum / sum | ?

2. If he runs too fast he will | lump / dump / bump | into us.

3. I will put a | bump / pump / lump | of coal in the fire.

Write the word that makes sense in the blank.

1. I can hear Jan _____ the [music notation] .   gum / hum / sum

2. _____ the [pump] from the well.   Lump / Jump / Pump

3. Ann likes to _____ rope with Judd.   jump / dump / pump

4. Did the bunny _____ his tail?   thump / lump / dump

131

Name _____ Date _____

Trace over the word three or four times. Next, write the word in the space provided.

This side for those who print.   This side for those who use cursive.

um   *um*

gum   *gum*

hum   *hum*

sum   *sum*

ump   *ump*

bump   *bump*

dump   *dump*

pump   *pump*

132

Name _____   Date _____

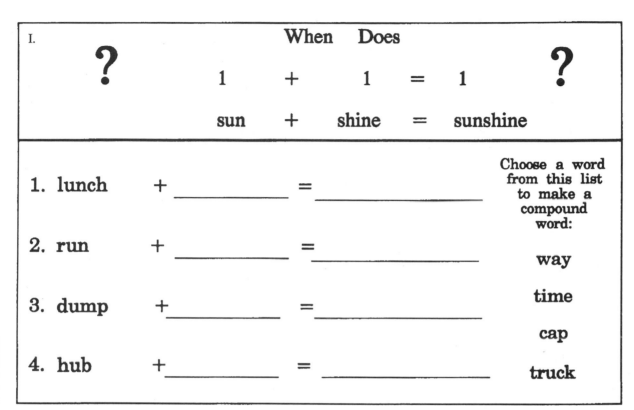

I.

? **When Does**

$$1 \quad + \quad 1 \quad = \quad 1$$

sun + shine = sunshine ?

1. lunch   + _____ = _____

2. run   + _____ = _____

3. dump   + _____ = _____

4. hub   + _____ = _____

Choose a word
from this list
to make a
compound
word:

way

time

cap

truck

II. Read each word.
Put a short mark or long mark above the first vowel.

Example: stŏp   rāin

1. shell   6. hill   11. weep   16. chest

2. sight   7. lame   12. time   17. main

3. cash   8. hump   13. shock   18. punch

4. lunch   9. cheat   14. pie   19. gum

5. mow   10. hole   15. bow   20. neck

Name _____ Date _____

I. Fill in the correct letter.

1. The ____um of 1 + 1 = 2 .   s   b   g

---

2. Do you like to ____ump rope?   th   j   b

---

3. We will take the trash to the ____ump.   b   d   j

---

4. We need a ____ump of coal for the fire.   l   h   p

---

5. I did not mean to ____ump in to you.   d   b   l

---

6. May I have a stick of ____um?   g   b   s

---

7. Jim will ____ump up the tire.   b   p   d

---

8. I can hear him ____um the .   s   h   g

© 1993 by Rosella Bernstein

II. Choose a word from the box and match it to the definition. Write it on the line.

jump	gum	thump
dump	bump	sum

1. It is sticky.   _____

2. A place for trash   _____

3. What you get when you add numbers   _____

4. A bunny can do this with his tail   _____

5. To leap is to   _____

6. To hit or run into   _____

134

Name _____   Date _____

1. Have the pupil go over the lists of words at the top of the exercise. Point out to the pupil that the ending of each word is the same. Examples: *cub rub tub*.
2. Next have the pupil do the exercise, crossing out the two words that are incorrect.
3. When all the sentences have been done in this way, the pupil returns to the first sentence and *orally* reads each sentence with the correct word.

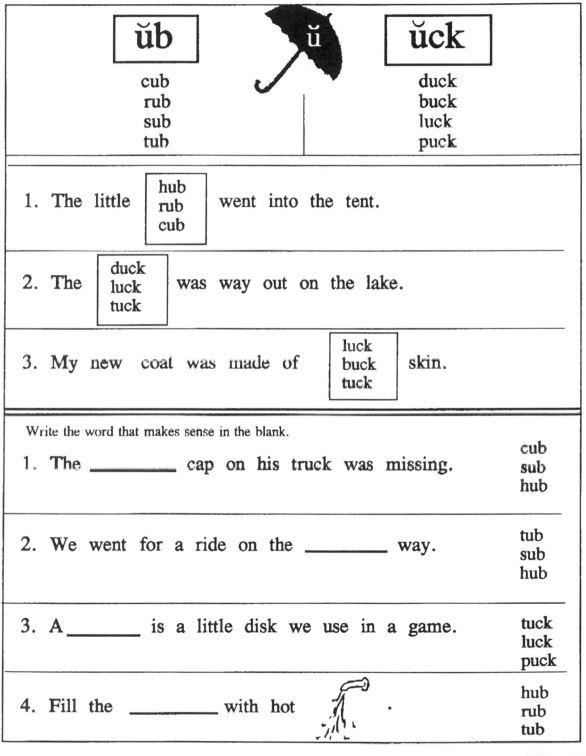

ŭb	ŭ	**ŭck**
cub		duck
rub		buck
sub		luck
tub		puck

1. The little [hub / rub / cub] went into the tent.

2. The [duck / luck / tuck] was way out on the lake.

3. My new coat was made of [luck / buck / tuck] skin.

Write the word that makes sense in the blank.

1. The _____ cap on his truck was missing.   cub sub hub

2. We went for a ride on the _____ way.   tub sub hub

3. A _____ is a little disk we use in a game.   tuck luck puck

4. Fill the _____ with hot .   hub rub tub

Trace over the word three or four times. Next, write the word in the space provided.

This side for those who print.   This side for those who use cursive.

ub   ub

cub   cub

rub   rub

tub   tub

uck   uck

duck   duck

luck   luck

truck   truck

I. Have the pupil mark the first vowel of each word with a long or short marking. Since these are multi-syllable words, work with the student and encourage him/her to read each word to see how many can be decoded.

1. sāilor

2. shŏpper

3. mailman

4. tepee

5. butter

6. toaster

7. dentist

8. lucky

9. apple

10. subway

11. window

12. toenail

13. cleaner

14. picnic

15. copper

16. rabbit

17. rubber

18. sideshow

II. These are difficult multisyllable words at this level. However, explain to the pupil that if he/she can figure out the part that is underlined and uses the context clues, it will be less difficult to decode the word. Practice helps.

1. A <u>duck</u>ling is a little duck.   duckling

2. A <u>truck</u>-load of hay will feed a lot of cattle.   truck-load

3. Tires are made of <u>rub</u>ber.   rubber

4. The ride on the <u>su</u>bway was a lot of fun.   subway

5. The soap <u>bub</u>ble broke when I laid my hand on it.   bubble

6. Was there a lot of <u>ru</u>bble in the cave?   rubble

137

Name _____   Date _____

I. ACROSS

→

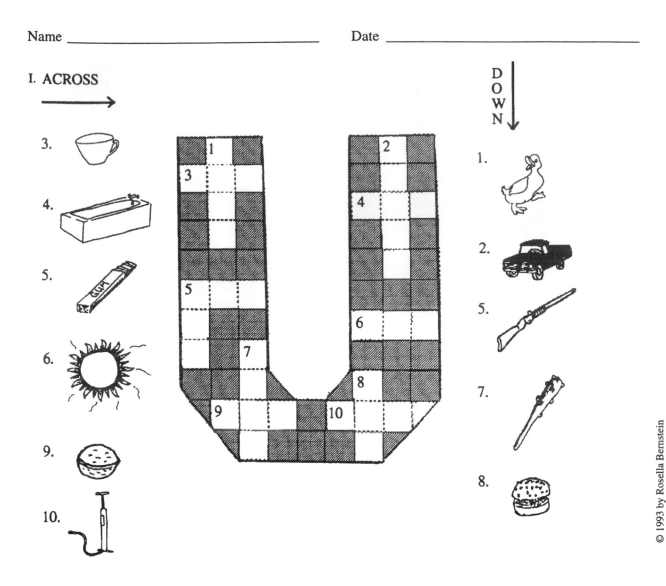

3.

4.

5.

6.

9.

10.

DOWN
↓

1.

2.

5.

7.

8.

II. See how many new words can be made by just changing the vowel:

Example: rub ⟶ _rib, rob_   ă   ĕ   ĭ   ŏ   ŭ

1. cub   ⟶   _____

2. tub   ⟶   _____

3. puck ⟶   _____

4. buck ⟶   _____

5. luck ⟶   _____

HUMPTY-DUMPTY

Humpty-Dumpty sat on a stump,

But Humpty-Dumpty didn't know how to jump.

So off the stump Humpty-Dumpty fell,

And from that bump got a crack in his shell.

The king's men could not get Humpty unstuck,

Humpty-Dumpty had very bad luck.

His shell did not mend,

So this is the end,

Of an egg that went thud in the mud.

The lesson is...................

Before you jump and get yourself in a muddle,

Take a good look or you may land in a puddle.

With practice this poem should take approximately one minute to read orally.

Name _____   Date _____

1. Have the pupil go over the lists of words at the top of the exercise. Point out to the pupil that the ending of each word is the same. Examples: *cub   rub   tub*.
2. Next have the pupil do the exercise, crossing out the two words that are incorrect.
3. When all the sentences have been done in this way, the pupil returns to the first sentence and *orally* reads each sentence with the correct word.

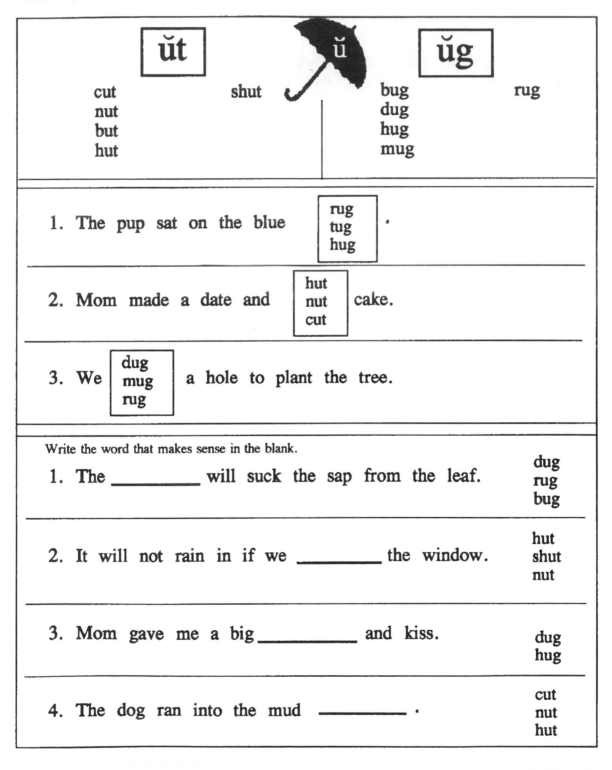

ŭt		ŭ	ŭg	
cut	shut		bug	rug
nut			dug	
but			hug	
hut			mug	

1. The pup sat on the blue
   | rug |
   | tug |
   | hug |
   .

2. Mom made a date and
   | hut |
   | nut |
   | cut |
   cake.

3. We
   | dug |
   | mug |
   | rug |
   a hole to plant the tree.

Write the word that makes sense in the blank.

1. The _____ will suck the sap from the leaf.   dug / rug / bug

2. It will not rain in if we _____ the window.   hut / shut / nut

3. Mom gave me a big _____ and kiss.   dug / hug

4. The dog ran into the mud _____ .   cut / nut / hut

140

Name _____ Date _____

Trace over the word three or four times. Next, write the word in the space provided.

This side for those who print.   This side for those who use cursive.

ut   ut

cut   cut

nut   nut

but   but

ug   ug

dug   dug

bug   bug

rug   rug

141

© 1993 by Rosella Bernstein

Name _____   Date _____

I. Write the name of the picture in the blank.
   Look for the word in the puzzle and draw a line around it.

a	q	e	t	i	c	e	w	r	g	i	a
p	r	u	g	x	n	f	k	s	b	t	x
j	d	h	d	u	p	d	u	c	k	y	r
c	s	g	b	u	c	a	l	u	w	m	v
u	k	q	l	u	n	u	t	x	b	f	c
p	u	y	k	h	f	g	w	l	j	u	g
a	n	b	u	d	e	o	m	v	t	e	z
d	r	u	y	r	s	q	c	u	t	i	n
n	m	g	f	j	u	o	g	h	k	p	o
z	t	s	h	i	n	v	q	l	p	j	z

II. In the following exercise, the pupil fills in the vowel that is shown at the top of each column. The first one has
    been done as an example. Then have the student read across each line.

ă	ĕ	ĭ	ŏ	ŭ
f a n		f i n		f u n
h __ t		h __ t	h __ t	h __ t
h __ m	h __ m	h __ m		h __ m
		r __ b	r __ b	r __ b
b __ t	b __ t	b __ t		b __ t
s __ ck		s __ ck	s __ ck	s __ ck
r __ g		r __ g		r __ g

142

Name _____   Date _____

1. Explain to the pupil that all the pictures on this page begin with the same vowel sound as the word **umbrella**.
2. Read the following definition to the pupil:
   Upper case letters are capital letters.
3. Next, the pupil names each picture and writes the name from the list.

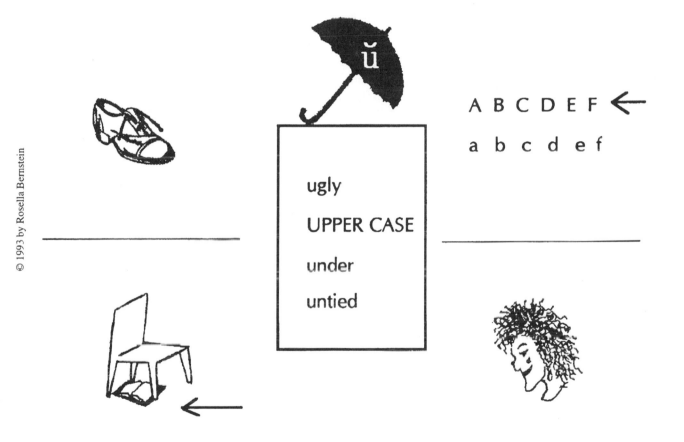

ugly

UPPER CASE

under

untied

_____

_____

_____

_____

Choose a word from one of these columns according to the letter under the blank in the story on the next page. Write it in the blank in the story. It can make sense or just be nonsensical. When this part of the exercise is completed, have the pupil read aloud the entire story.

A	B	C	D	E
bench	bright	sad	wife	five
chair	sunny	mad	dog	three
mat	hot	silly	cat	six
rug	fine	happy	pet	seven
tub	rainy	funny	duck	nine
rock				ten

F	G	H	I	J
pot	rocks	night	fox	hash
pail	bats	day	rat	meat
pan	chains	week	pig	ham
sack	shells	year	hog	
plate	bones			
bowl	weeds			

K	L	M
red	fat	cried
blue	skinny	laughed
green	big	yelled
yellow	little	smiled
black	ugly	
white	pretty	

A _____ TALE
C

One _____ and _____ _____, an old
       B   B   H

man said to his _____,
                    D

"Come, let us bake some _____."
                               J

They put it into a big _____.
                              F

Then the man said, "This will be better if we add _____
                                                          E

_____ _____."
      K   G

And so they added them.

The man said, "This still needs some _____."
                                             G

He added them.

They let it bake all _____ in the sun. It got hot.
                            H

At last the man said, "It is time to sit down and eat."

They sat down on a _____ _____ .
                          K   A

The man filled a big _____ dish.
                            K

"I will take a bite, then you take a bite," said the old man.

But just then, a _____ _____ came and ate it
                        L   I

all up.

The old man did not get a bite.

His _____ did not get a bite.
         D

They were _____ .
                 C

They just sat there and _____ all _____ .
                               M   H

And that is the end of this _____ tale.
                                   C

CHECK LIST

ŭ

bun	cub	dump	fun	gun
bunch	cut	duck		gum
bum	cuff	dug		
bump				
buck				
but				
bug				

hub	jump	lunch	munch	nut
hut		luck	mud	
huff			muff	
hug			mutt	
hum				
hump				
hunch				

punch	run	sun	tub
pump	rub	sum	tug
puck	rug	sub	truck
puff		suck	thump

Select a word and have the pupil attempt to read it. (Don't select more than a total of ten words a session.)
If the pupil is able to read the word, put a plus (+) mark in front of the word.
If the pupil is not able to read the word, put a minus (-) mark and change it into a plus when the pupil can recognize it.
Make flash cards of the unsuccessful words for practice.

Name _____   Date _____

I. Have the pupil go over the lists of words at the top of the page. Here are two possible ways the long *u* is made. (Another way will be presented in the next lesson.)

1. Vowel *u* followed by any consonant followed by vowel *e*. Example: vcv *cube*

2. Vowel *u* followed immediately by the vowel *e*. Example: vv *fuel*

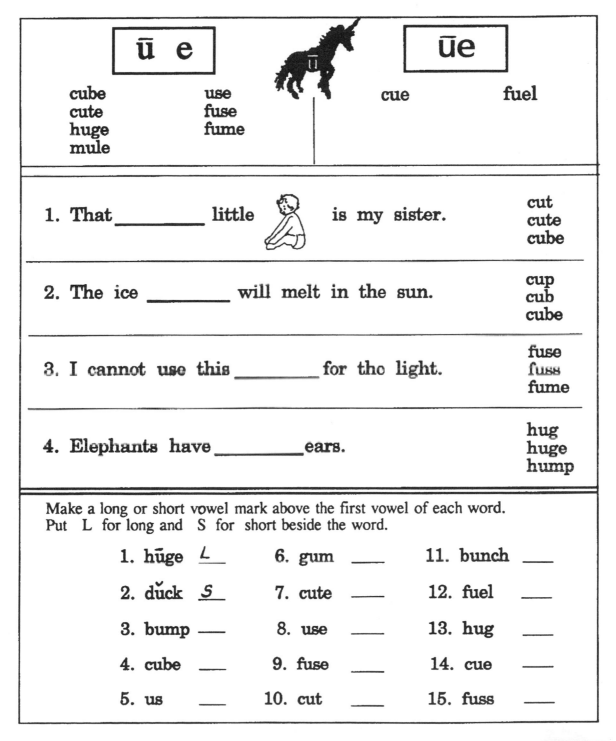

ū e		ūe
cube use		cue fuel
cute fuse		
huge fume		
mule		

1. That _____ little [child] is my sister.
   - cut
   - cute
   - cube

2. The ice _____ will melt in the sun.
   - cup
   - cub
   - cube

3. I cannot use this _____ for the light.
   - fuse
   - fuss
   - fume

4. Elephants have _____ ears.
   - hug
   - huge
   - hump

Make a long or short vowel mark above the first vowel of each word.
Put L for long and S for short beside the word.

1. hūge *L*   6. gum ___   11. bunch ___

2. dŭck *S*   7. cute ___   12. fuel ___

3. bump ___   8. use ___   13. hug ___

4. cube ___   9. fuse ___   14. cue ___

5. us ___   10. cut ___   15. fuss ___

147

Name _____   Date _____

Trace over the word three or four times. Next, write the word in the space provided.

This side for those who print.   This side for those who use cursive.

cute   *cute*

cube   *cube*

use   *use*

huge   *huge*

fuel   *fuel*

cue   *cue*

I.

UNSCRAMBLER

euml   ebcu   sefu   ughe

_____   _____   _____   _____

tecu   sue   ufem   eful

_____   _____   _____   _____

II.

A-MAZE-ING

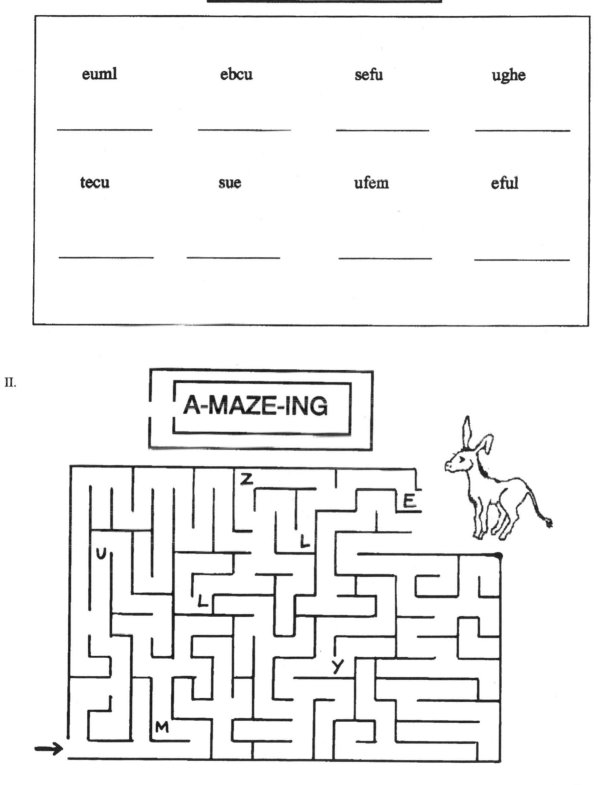

_ _ _ _ _ _ _

duck	thump	run	hut	mule
bunch	jump	luck	lunch	cute
fuel	gum	**ū**	dump	fuse
bug	lunch	tub	bump	huge
use	dug	sum	rug	cube

I. Put a short or long mark on the first vowel of each word. Find the line (across, down, or diagonal) that is BINGO—all short vowel words or all long vowel words. Write the BINGO words on the lines below.

_____

_____

_____

_____

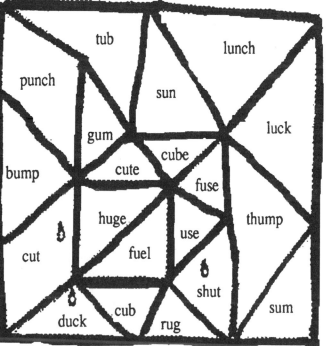

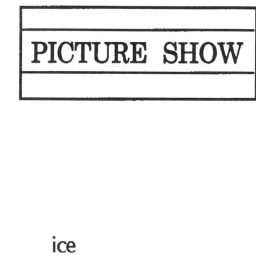

PICTURE SHOW

ice

_____

II. To find the picture, color blue all the sections containing a long *u* word.

Long <u>u</u> Words That Do Not Need a Vowel Helper

cū pid.............cupid
Cū ba..............Cuba
hū man.........human
pū pil..............pupil
mū sic.............music
mū seum........museum
bū gle.............bugle
fū ture..........future

ū ni form...........uniform
ū ni corn...........unicorn
ū ni cy cle.........unicycle

Practice reading these sentences:

1. The band plays nice music.

2. We have a new pupil in the math class.

3. The new pupil wore his band uniform.

4. Cupid is not a human being.

5. A unicorn is not a real animal.

6. The future is not what is happening now.
   The future is not what happened before.
   The future is what will happen in time to come.

7. I saw a man ride a unicycle today.

8. The man was from Cuba.

9. The man played a bugle at the same time that he rode

   his unicycle.

10. We went to the museum to see the dinosaurs.

Name _____ Date _____

I. Write the word on the blank that goes with each group of words on the left.

1. Has a shape like a box _____ | uniform

2. Very big in size _____ | cube

3. Has notes _____ | pupil

4. What members of a band dress in _____ | huge

5. Can add and say ABC's _____ | unicorn

6. An animal that is not real _____ | unicycle

7. Needed to make lights go on _____ | music

8. Has one wheel _____ | fuse

II. Ask the pupil to write a short story and include the words that are in the box below. If the pupil is unable to write the story him- or herself, print it for the pupil on these lines. Next tell the pupil to underline all the long *u* words in the story.
Last, have the pupil practice reading the story so that he or she can read it fluently.

| uniform | music | bugle | pupil | museum |

_____

_____

_____

_____

_____

_____

_____

152

Name _____   Date _____

CHECK LIST

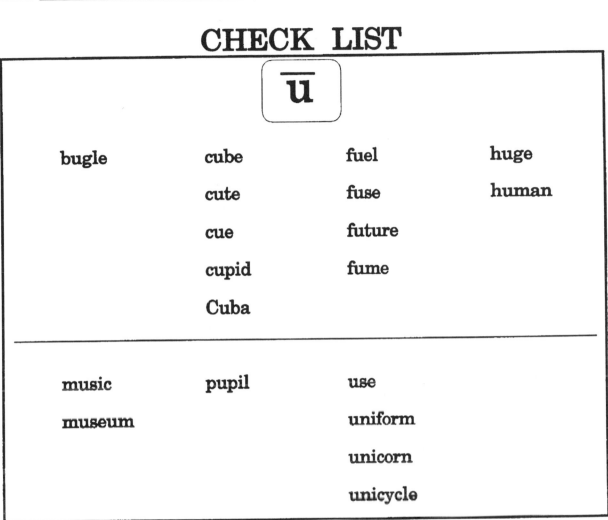

ū			
bugle	cube	fuel	huge
	cute	fuse	human
	cue	future	
	cupid	fume	
	Cuba		

music	pupil	use
museum		uniform
		unicorn
		unicycle

Select a word and have the pupil attempt to read it. (Don't select more than a total of ten words a session.)
If the pupil is able to read the word, put a plus (+) mark in front of the word.
If the pupil is not able to read the word, put a minus (-) mark and change it into a plus when the pupil can recognize it.
Make flash cards of the unsuccessful words for practice.

PART TWO

Activities for Irregular
Vowel Combinations
Diphthongs
R–Controlled Vowels

IRREGULAR VOWEL COMBINATIONS

ô

o͝o

o͞o

ĕ

ā

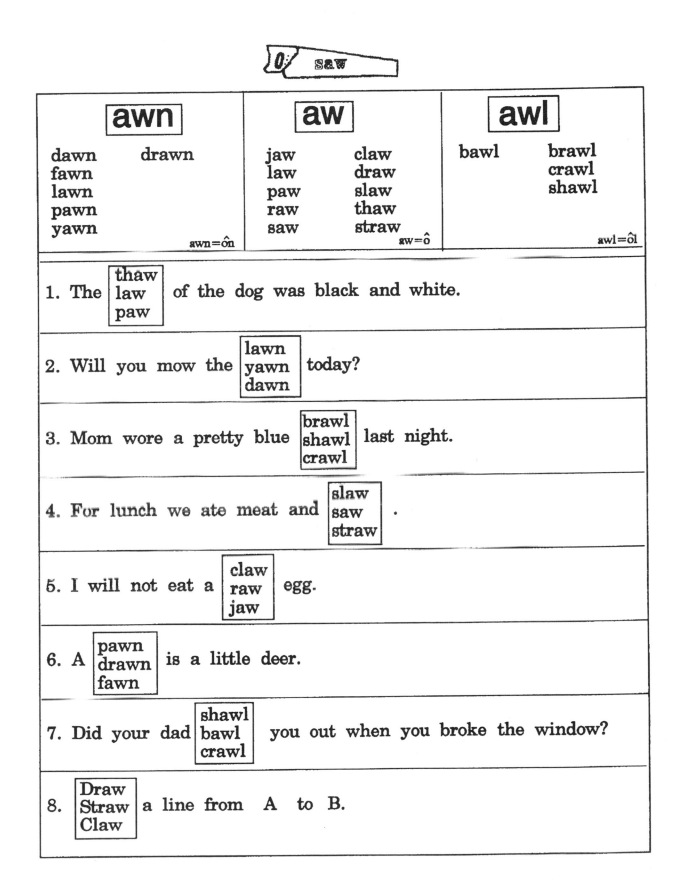

awn	**aw**	**awl**
dawn drawn fawn lawn pawn yawn awn=ôn	jaw claw law draw paw slaw raw thaw saw straw aw=ô	bawl brawl crawl shawl awl=ôl

1. The ⎡thaw / law / paw⎤ of the dog was black and white.

2. Will you mow the ⎡lawn / yawn / dawn⎤ today?

3. Mom wore a pretty blue ⎡brawl / shawl / crawl⎤ last night.

4. For lunch we ate meat and ⎡slaw / saw / straw⎤ .

5. I will not eat a ⎡claw / raw / jaw⎤ egg.

6. A ⎡pawn / drawn / fawn⎤ is a little deer.

7. Did your dad ⎡shawl / bawl / crawl⎤ you out when you broke the window?

8. ⎡Draw / Straw / Claw⎤ a line from A to B.

Name _____

Date _____

aw

For those who print

1.

2.

she saw   we draw

For those who use cursive.

1.

2.

160

Name _____   Date _____

Each underlined word has the *aw* sound in it as in *hawk*.
Together with the context clues, the students should attempt to figure out the underlined word and read the complete sentence.

1. I have an <u>awful</u> sore on my lip.   awful

2. The <u>awning</u> will keep the sun out.   awning

3. The <u>hawk</u> has a beak, claws, and good sight.   hawk

4. Dawn put a <u>strawberry</u> on top of the ice cream.   strawberry

5. Don't stand there and <u>gawk</u> at me.   gawk

1. The student names each picture and writes the word for that picture.
2. Then the student draws a line around the word in the puzzle below. Hint: The words may go across or down.

a	e	d	p	f	e	l	c	l	a	w
p	a	w	c	d	m	o	a	v	m	o
r	h	l	v	l	u	y	i	b	t	p
z	i	g	s	a	w	j	r	c	g	s
q	e	c	h	o	n	k	a	u	b	t
c	d	s	a	b	h	t	z	k	x	r
w	a	c	w	j	r	a	s	f	v	a
r	z	h	l	t	k	s	q	i	o	w
i	b	j	x	w	f	h	s	x	g	e
n	f	m	y	p	h	a	w	k	o	m
j	q	y	m	k	w	n	l	g	n	z

Name _____   Date _____

I.

aul	AUGUST	**ause**
haul maul Paul		pause cause

aul = ôl   ause = ôz

1. | Maul
Paul
Haul | is the name of my dad.

2. Keep away from that big cat. It might | Paul
haul
maul | you.

3. This truck can | haul
maul
Paul | a lot of trash.

4. We can | cause
pause | and rest here.

5. Did the slick road | pause
cause | the truck to crash?

© 1993 by Rosella Bernstein

II.

The student reads the first part of the sentence and decides how it should be finished. If he/she can't write it, then the instructor should print it out. When all the sentences have been completed the student rereads them.

1. Paul will go to _____

2. The train will haul _____

3. We will pause and rest by _____

Name _____

Date _____

aul

For those who print

1.

We haul

2.

It's Paul

For those who use cursive.

1.

2.

163

1. Explain to the pupil that all the pictures in the exercise below begin with the same vowel sound *au* as in the word *autograph.*
2. Read the following definitions to the pupil as you point to the picture:
   a. Australia is a country and a continent. It is located just below the equator with the Indian Ocean on the left and the South Pacific Ocean on the right.
   b. An auger is a tool for boring holes in wood.
   c. An automat is a restaurant where food is gotten from compartments that open when coins are put into slots.
   d. An auk is a chunky, short-winged sea bird that lives in the arctic region.
3. Next, the pupil names each picture (some words may be new, so give help here) and writes the name from the list.

*AU*TOGRAPH

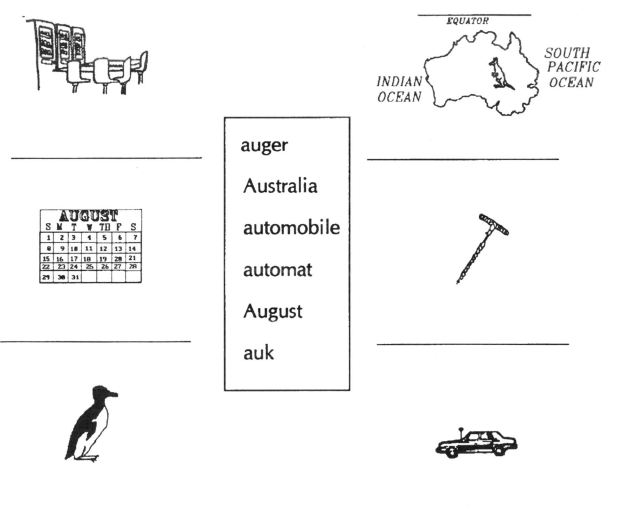

auger

Australia

automobile

automat

August

auk

I.

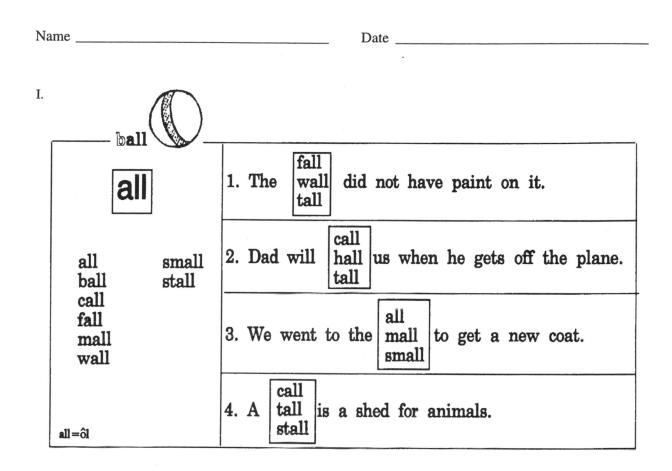

b**all**

all

all   small
ball   stall
call
fall
mall
wall

all = ôl

1. The | fall / wall / tall | did not have paint on it.

2. Dad will | call / hall / tall | us when he gets off the plane.

3. We went to the | all / mall / small | to get a new coat.

4. A | call / tall / stall | is a shed for animals.

II.

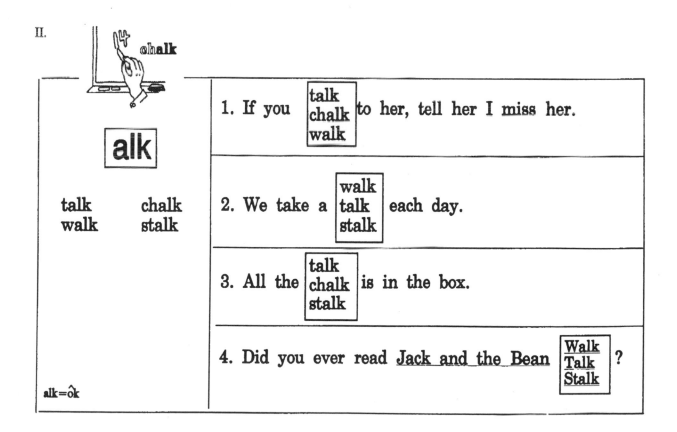

chalk

alk

talk   chalk
walk   stalk

alk = ôk

1. If you | talk / chalk / walk | to her, tell her I miss her.

2. We take a | walk / talk / stalk | each day.

3. All the | talk / chalk / stalk | is in the box.

4. Did you ever read Jack and the Bean | Walk / Talk / Stalk | ?

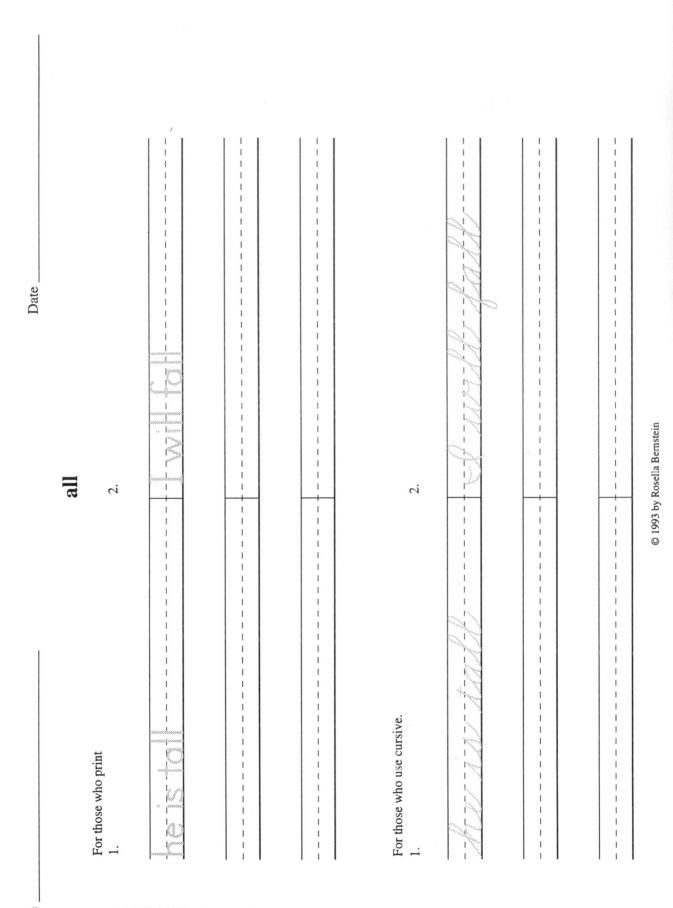

Name _____   Date _____

all

For those who print

1.

2.

For those who use cursive.

1.

2.

Name _____ Date _____

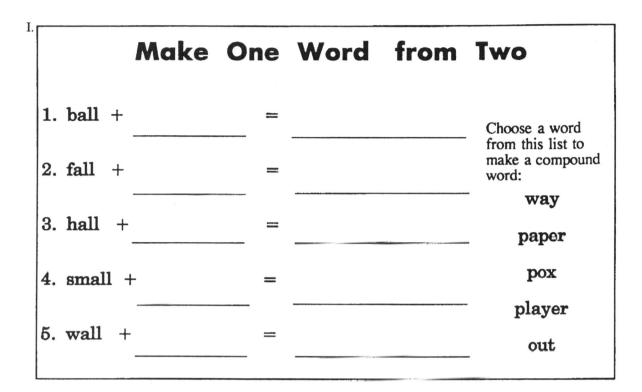

I.

Make One Word from Two

1. ball + _____ = _____

2. fall + _____ = _____

3. hall + _____ = _____

4. small + _____ = _____

5. wall + _____ = _____

Choose a word from this list to make a compound word:

way

paper

pox

player

out

II.

unscramblers

kalw   hckla   lahl

_____   _____   _____

atlk   abll   stlak

_____   _____   _____

I.

aught	1. Dad [taught / caught] a fish in the lake.
	2. He [taught / caught] me how to clean the fish.
caught taught	3. Dad [caught / taught] me how to swim.
aught=ôt	

II.

ought	1. Dad [thought / bought / brought] the fish home.
	2. Mom [bought / fought / ought] me a saw. Now I can cut some logs.
bought brought fought thought ought	3. I [brought / thought / ought] that was very nice of her.
	4. The dogs [fought / bought / brought] over some bones.
	5. It is late. I [thought / bought / ought] to go home now.
	6. Dan [ought / bought / brought] his pet snake to school.
ought=ôt	7. The boys [fought / bought / ought] over a small ball.

Name _____

Date _____

aught

For those who print

1.  I caught

2.  she taught

For those who use cursive.

1. 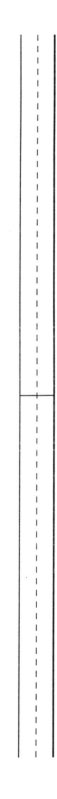 I caught she taught

Name _____   Date _____

CHECK LIST

aw

aw = ô

bawl	fawn	saw
brawl	jaw	shawl
claw	law	slaw
crawl	lawn	straw
dawn	paw	thaw
draw	pawn	yawn
drawn	raw	

Additional Words with this aw sound:

awful
awkward
awning
crawfish
gawk
hawk
squaw
strawberry

all

all = ôl

all	mall
ball	small
call	stall
fall	tall
hall	wall

Additional Words with this all sound:

swallow
wallet
wallop
wallow

alk

alk = ôk

chalk

stalk

talk

walk

Additional words with this alk sound:

chalkboard
talkathon
talkfest

CHECK LIST

au

$au = \hat{o}$

cause

haul

maul

Paul

pause

Additional Words that have this au *sound:*

auditorium	autumn
August	caution
Australia	exhaust
author	fault
autograph	saucer
automat	sausage
automobile	

aught

$aught = \hat{o}t$

caught

taught

Additional Words that have this aught *sound:*

daughter
haughty......too proud of oneself
onslaught....attack
slaughter.....killing of an animal

ought

$ought = \hat{o}t$

bought

brought

fought

ought

thought

Additional Words that have this ought *sound:*

sought after......in demand
drought..........long period of dry weather
wrought iron

ook		**ood**
book brook		good stood
cook shook		hood
hook		wood
look		
ook=ŏŏk took		ood=ŏŏd

1. Open your
| book |
| look |
| nook |
to page 24.

2. The fish was caught with a
| hook |
| look |
| nook |
.

3. We
| book |
| brook |
| shook |
the bag and the frog fell out.

4. Our teacher
| hook |
| took |
| book |
us out to play.

5. We sat under a tree by the
| brook |
| shook |
| look |
.

6. Ann will
| nook |
| look |
| cook |
dinner for you and me.

7.
| Cook |
| Look |
| Book |
under the rug for the pin.

8. We will sit in the
| look |
| hook |
| nook |
and read a book.

Name _____

Date _____

ook

For those who print

1. you took

2. she can cook

For those who use cursive.

1. you took

2. she can cook

I.

bulldog   **ull**

bull
full
pull

ull = o͝ol

1. The bag is _____ of candy.

pull
full

2. _____ the 🐘 over here.

Pull
Bull
Full

3. Did you see the _____ fight?

full
pull
bull

II.

ould

could
would
should

ould = o͝od

The pupil reads the first part of the sentence and decides how to finish it.
 If the pupil cannot write the rest of the sentence the instructor writes it for him/her.
When all the sentences are finished the pupil reads all the completed sentences.

1. Paul could win the race if _____

2. Would you please get _____

3. We should help our _____

Name _____

Date _____

ull

For those who print

1. we pull

2. it is full

For those who use cursive.

1.

2.

175

CHECK LIST

oo

$oo = \breve{oo}$

book	hood
brook	look
cook	nook
crook	shook
foot	stood
good	took
hook	wood

Additional words that have this oo sound:

football	footstep
foothold	good-bye
footlight	goodness
footlocker	hooky
footnote	soot.....a black dust-like material
footprint	woof....barking sound of dog family
footrest	wool

ould

$ould = \breve{oo}d$

would

could

should

ull

$ull = \breve{oo}l$

bull

full

pull

Additional words that have this ull sound:

bully

pulley.....a wheel with a v-shaped rim by which a
        rope turns it

pullet......a young hen

moon

oo	oon	ool
boo coo moo zoo	moon spoon noon soon	cool spool fool pool tool
$oo=\overline{oo}$	$oon-\overline{oo}n$	$ool=\overline{oo}l$

1. The man said the | moon / noon / soon | is made of cheese.

2. I will get the | pool / tool / cool | and fix my bike.

3. We can go to the | boo / zoo / coo | today.

4. I like to dive into the | tool / pool / fool | when it is not too cool.

5. Dan will meet us today at | soon / loon / noon | .

6. Did Jim | pool / fool / cool | you with his new trick?

7. Soon the ____ will eat with a | soon / spoon / noon | .

8. A | loose / noose / moose | is a big animal.

Name _____

Date _____

oon

For those who print

1. It is noon

2. See you soon

For those who use cursive.

1. *It is noon*

2. *See you soon*

I.

oup

soup
croup
group

oup = o͞op

The pupil reads the first part of the sentence and decides how to finish it.
If the pupil cannot write the rest of the sentence the instructor writes it for him/her.
When all the sentences are finished the pupil reads all the completed sentences.

1. This soup is_____

2. A group of us went to _____

3. My_____ has the croup.

II.

All the following scrambled words have the   oo   sound.
Rearrange the letters to make a word.

lopo   osup   romo

_____   _____   _____

grpou   olof   nono

_____   _____   _____

Name _____

Date _____

oup

For those who print

1.   not soup

2.   a group

For those who use cursive.

1.   *hot soup*

2.   *a group*

HIDE 'N SEEK

Draw a line around the hidden picture and write the number on it.

1. goose
2. hoop
3. spool

4. broom
5. spoon
6. moon

7. boot
8. moose
9. noose

ew

dew	chew
new	crew
	flew
	knew
	screw
	stew
	threw

screw

ew = $\bar{oo}$

1. The plane
dew
flew
knew
with a crew of five.

2. Mom bought me a
flew
new
knew
coat today.

3. Did the dog
chew
brew
threw
on the big bone?

4. Small drops of
dew
drew
new
were on the grass.

5. Mike
brew
stew
threw
the ball to Pat.

6. Do you like to eat
chew
stew
screw
?

7. Rick
crew
knew
drew
a funny face on his cap.

8. I will
brew
flew
crew
some tea for you.

© 1993 by Rosella Bernstein

Name _____   Date _____

ew

For those who print

1.

2.

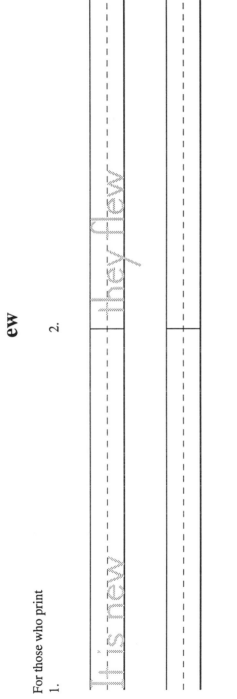

For those who use cursive.

1.

2.

I. Write the missing letters on the blanks.

1. We ate _____ew for supper.   st   fl   ch

2. Ann _____ew the ball to Paul.   dr   thr   ch

3. It is not raining but there is some _____ew.   d   dr   cr

4. We will not eat the _____oup now.   gr   s   cr

   It is too hot.

5. Our _____oup will camp here tonight.   cr   s   gr

6. Rick is sick at home today.

   He has the _____oup.   gr   cr   s

II.

DOT-TO-DOT

_____   _____

_____   _____

184

I.

JUNE

1	2	3	4
5	6	7	8	9	10	11
12	13	14	15	16	17	18
19	20	21	22	23	24	25
26	27	28	29	30

une

June   prune
tune
dune

une = ōōn

1. I will hum a little [tune / June / prune] on my kazoo.

2. Jim will be five in May.
   Jane will be five in [prune / June / tune] .

3. A [dune / June / tune] is a heap of sand made by wind.

II.

ue

due   blue
Sue   glue
           clue
           true

ue = ōō

1. The [glue / blue / true] will help the tag stick to the box.

2. The gas bill is [glue / clue / due] today.

3. Sue has on a [due / glue / blue] dress.

III.

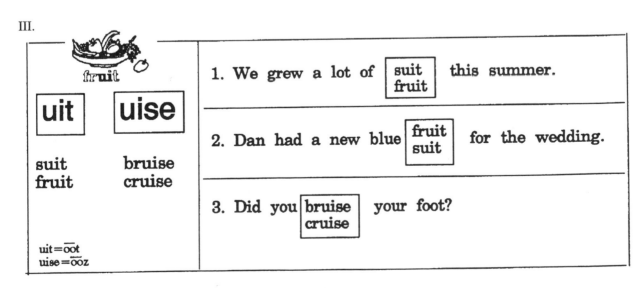

fruit

uit   **uise**

suit   bruise
fruit   cruise

uit = ōōt
uise = ōōz

1. We grew a lot of [suit / fruit] this summer.

2. Dan had a new blue [fruit / suit] for the wedding.

3. Did you [bruise / cruise] your foot?

185

Name _____

Date _____

ue

For those who print

1. It is blue

2. we will glue

For those who use cursive.

1.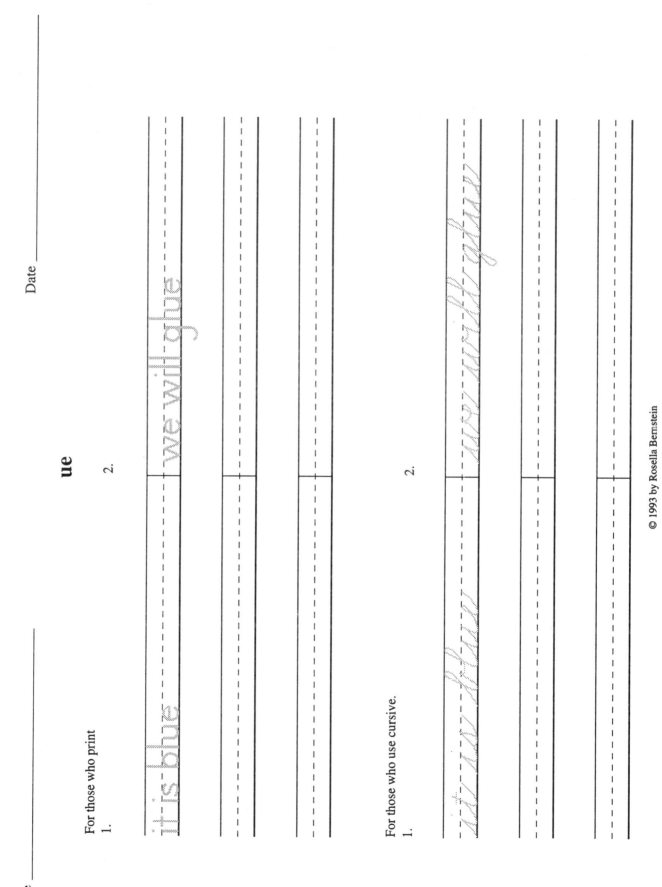

2.

Name _____

Date _____

uit

For those who print

1. new suit

2. good fruit

For those who use cursive.

1. new suit

2. good fruit

I.

> Each underlined word has the ue sound as in **blue.**
> Together with the context clues, the student should try to decode the underlined word and read the complete sentence.
>
> 1. A <u>flue</u> is a pipe or tube that lets smoke out.   flue
>
> 2. The men fought a <u>duel</u> at sunrise.   duel
>
> 3. Do not be <u>cruel</u> to animals.   cruel

II.

> Each underlined word has the ui sound as in **fruit.**
> Together with the context clues, the student should try to decode the underlined word and read the complete sentence.
>
> 1. Jan fell and got a <u>bruise</u> on her arm.   bruise
>
> 2. We will go on a big boat for our <u>cruise</u> to Mexico.   cruise
>
> 3. Do you like <u>juice</u> with your meal?   juice

III.

> Draw a line around the word or words on the right that <u>rhyme</u> with the word on the left.

new	blue	soup	chew	noon
June	tune	prune	suit	jean
zoo	zap	stew	hoop	glue
boot	fruit	boat	root	pool

In A Big Stew

"I'll cook something good," I said to friend Ann.

So I got out a spoon and a huge old black pan.

We looked in the cookbook to try something new.

And ended up making a big pot of stew.

As I hummed a soft <u>tune</u> I threw in a <u>prune</u>,

A slice of fat <u>goose</u> and some strawberry <u>juice</u>.

I shook in some salt, black pepper, and spice.

I even threw in a little brown rice.

And when I was through with making the stew,

I gave some to Ann and tried the stew, too.

But a look at Ann's face and I instantly knew

That Ann was not keen on this something called "stew."

Now I have not a clue as to what I should do.

As to what I should do with this huge pot of stew.

SAY!!   How would you like to come over for lunch?

I'll even throw in a glass of pink punch!

CHECK LIST

oo

oo = $\overline{oo}$

boot	fool	moon	spool
boom	goose	moose	spoon
bloom	gloom	noon	stool
broom	groom	noose	stoop
coop	hoop	moose	toot
cool	hoot	pool	zoo
doom	loom	room	zoom
drool	loon	root	
droop	loop	soon	
food	loose	school	

Additional words that have this oo *sound:*

booby prize	goofy
booby trap	noodle
boost	poodle
choose	roost
doodad	rooster
doodle	woozy
gooey	yoo-hoo

ou

ou = $\overline{oo}$

croup

group

soup

Additional words that have this ou *sound:*

cougar......mountain lion. Member of the cat family
coupon
crouton.....toasted cube of dried bread used in soups and salads
louver...... an opening with slanted boards
mouton......sheep's fur made to look like beaver

ew

ew = $\overline{oo}$

brew	flew	threw
chew	knew	
crew	new	
dew	screw	
drew	stew	

Additional words that have this ew *sound :*

jewelry
newspaper
screwdriver
stewardess

© 1993 by Rosella Bernstein

CHECK LIST

ue

ue = $\overline{oo}$

blue   glue

clue   Sue

due   true

flue

Additional words that have this ue *sound:*

cruel
duel

u_e

u_e = $\overline{oo}$

June

prune

tune

Additional words that have this u_e *sound:*

dune.........a sand hill formed by the wind
dupe.........trick, deceive
lube.........oil used to make machinery run smoothly
rule
tube

ui

ui = $\overline{oo}$

fruit

suit

Additional words that have this ui *sound:*

bruise   recruit
cruise
juice

feather

ead	ealth	eath	eather
head bread dead dread read tread thread spread	health wealth	death breath	feather leather weather
ead=ĕd	ealth=ĕlth	eath=ĕth	eather=ĕther

1. We will get a loaf of wheat _____ at the store.

    dread
    bread
    tread

2. Did the _____ map show snow?

    weather
    leather
    feather

3. The cold air made her _____ look like steam.

    breath
    bread

4. We _____ butter and jam on our bread.

    thread
    spread
    dread

5. Eat good food and it will make your_____ better.

    wealth
    health

6. The bird has one big white _____ .

    feather
    leather
    weather

7. The book was so good I _____ it three times.

    head
    read
    dead

8. Did you use brown _____ on your leather jacket?

    dread
    tread
    thread

Name _____

Date _____

ead

For those who print

1. on his head

2. wheat bread

For those who use cursive.

1. on his head

2. wheat bread

Draw a picture for each word.

head

thread

bedspread

feather

nice weather

sweater

CHECK LIST

ea

ea = ŏ

bread	lead	weather
breath	leather	
dead	read	
death	spread	
feather	thread	
head	tread	
health	wealth	

Additional words that have this **ea** *sound:*

already	meadow	sweat
breakfast	measure	sweater
headache	peasant	threat
heavy	pleasant	treasure
instead	ready	weapon
jealous	steady	

sleigh

eigh	eight	ein
weigh sleigh	eight freight weight	vein rein
eigh = ā	eight = āt	ein = ān

Before starting the exercise below explain these definitions:
1. rein.........a long narrow strap by which to guide an animal
2. sleigh......a carriage mounted on runners for use on snow or ice, pulled by one or more horses
3. freight.....goods carried by a vehicle

1. We can ship this ☐ freight / eight ☐ by train, track, or plane.

2. Blood flows through the ☐ reins / veins ☐ to the ♥ .
heart

3. Dan is ☐ weight / eight ☐ years old today.

4. How much do you ☐ weigh / weight ☐ ?

5. Before the race started the man took the ☐ reins / veins ☐ in his hands.

6. From far off we could hear the ☐ weigh / sleigh ☐ bells.

7. The nurse put my ☐ eight / weight ☐ on the chart.

Name _____

Date _____

eight

For those who print

1. he is eight

2. your weight

For those who use cursive.

1. _[handwriting practice lines]_

2. _[handwriting practice lines]_

I. | Put the letter that explains the meaning of the word on the blank space.

A. The number after seven _____ ate

B. Past tense of eat _____ eight

A. How heavy something is _____ weight

B. To delay _____ wait

A. A strap to guide an animal _____ rein

B. Drops of water falling on earth _____ rain

A. A carriage on runners _____ slay

B. To kill _____ sleigh

II.

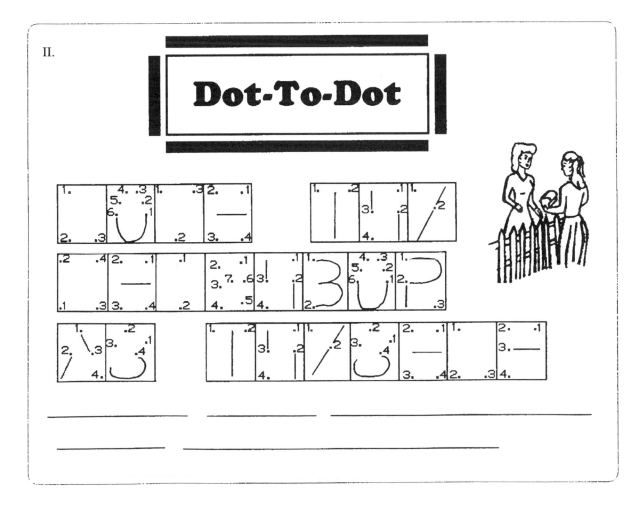

Dot-To-Dot

_____   _____

_____   _____

I.

eak

eak

steak

break

eak = āk

Read these sentences.

1. This <u>steak</u> is good.

2. Let's have more <u>steak.</u>

3. Let's take a <u>break.</u>

4. Did Meg <u>break</u> the dish?

II.

Put the letter that explains the meaning on the blank space.

A. A slice of meat   _____ stake

B. A post in the ground   _____ steak

A. Come apart   _____ break

B. Something that holds back a wheel   _____ brake

A. Very good   _____ great

B. A frame to hold a fire   _____ grate

Name _____

Date _____

eak

For those who print

1. don't break

2. it's a steak

For those who use cursive.

1. *don't break*

2. *it's a steak*

CHECK LIST

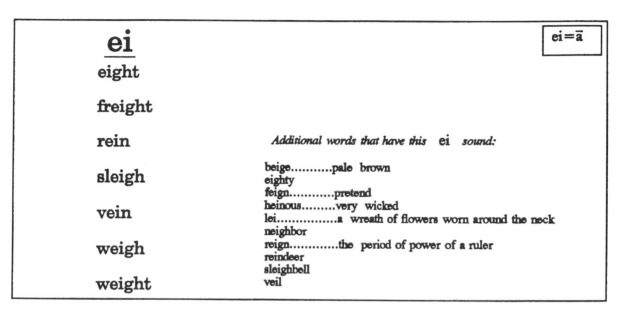

ei

ei=ā

eight

freight

rein

sleigh

vein

weigh

weight

Additional words that have this ei *sound:*

beige...........pale brown
eighty
feign............pretend
heinous.........very wicked
lei................a wreath of flowers worn around the neck
neighbor
reign.............the period of power of a ruler
reindeer
sleighbell
veil

eak

eak=āk

break

steak

Additional word with the ea *sound:*

great

DIPHTHONGS

ou

oi

Name _____   Date _____

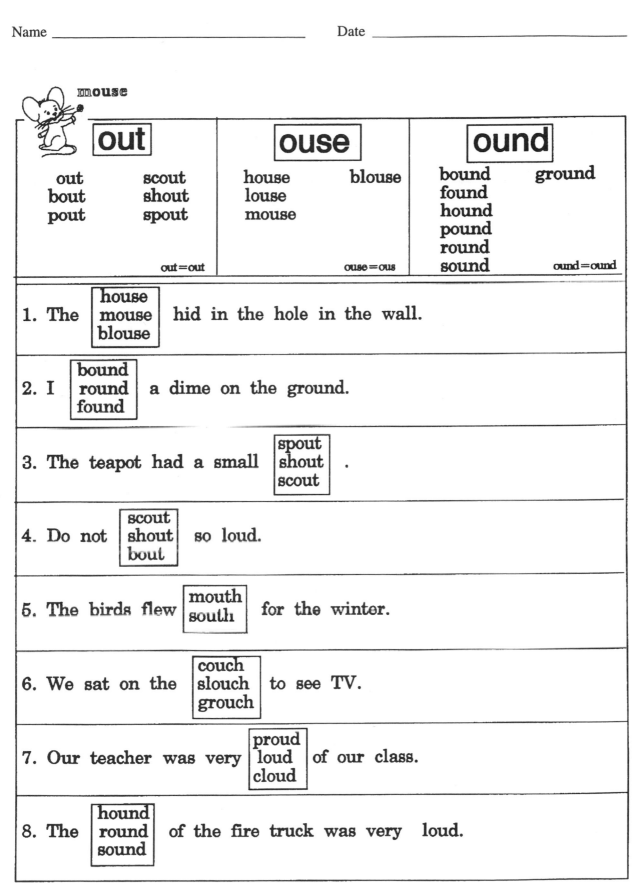

mouse

out	**ouse**	**ound**
out scout	house blouse	bound ground
bout shout	louse	found
pout spout	mouse	hound
		pound
		round
out = out	ouse = ous	sound ound = ound

1. The [house / mouse / blouse] hid in the hole in the wall.

2. I [bound / round / found] a dime on the ground.

3. The teapot had a small [spout / shout / scout] .

4. Do not [scout / shout / bout] so loud.

5. The birds flew [mouth / south] for the winter.

6. We sat on the [couch / slouch / grouch] to see TV.

7. Our teacher was very [proud / loud / cloud] of our class.

8. The [hound / round / sound] of the fire truck was very loud.

205

Name _____

Date _____

out

For those who print

1.

come out

2.

good scout

For those who use cursive.

1.

come out

2.

good scout

Name _____

Date _____

ouse

For those who print

1.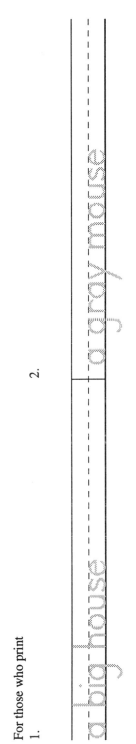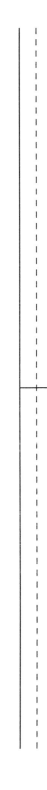

2.

For those who use cursive.

1.

2.

207

Name _____   Date _____

I. Each underlined word has the   **ou**   sound   as in **out.**
Together with the context clues, the student should try to decode the underlined word and read the complete sentence.

1. The <u>mountain</u> had a lot of snow on its peak.   mountain

2. Throw a penny into the <u>fountain.</u>   fountain

3. Today is a <u>cloudy</u> day.   cloudy

4. A <u>thousand</u> men fought in the battle.   thousand

5. Did you <u>count</u> how many books you have now?   count

II.

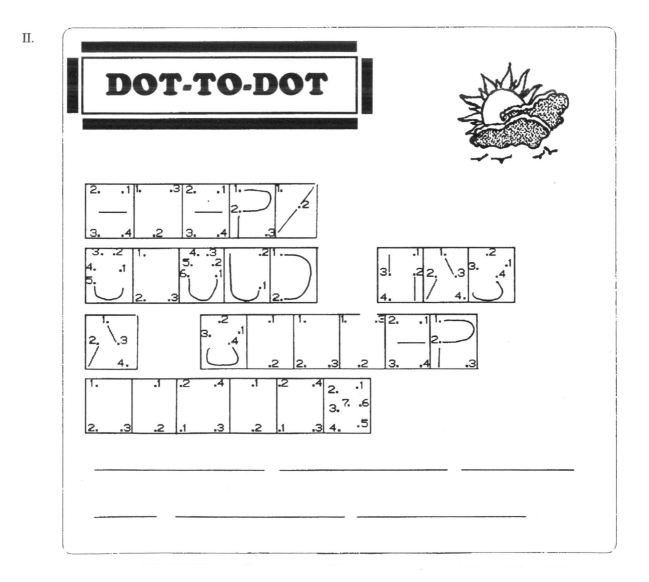

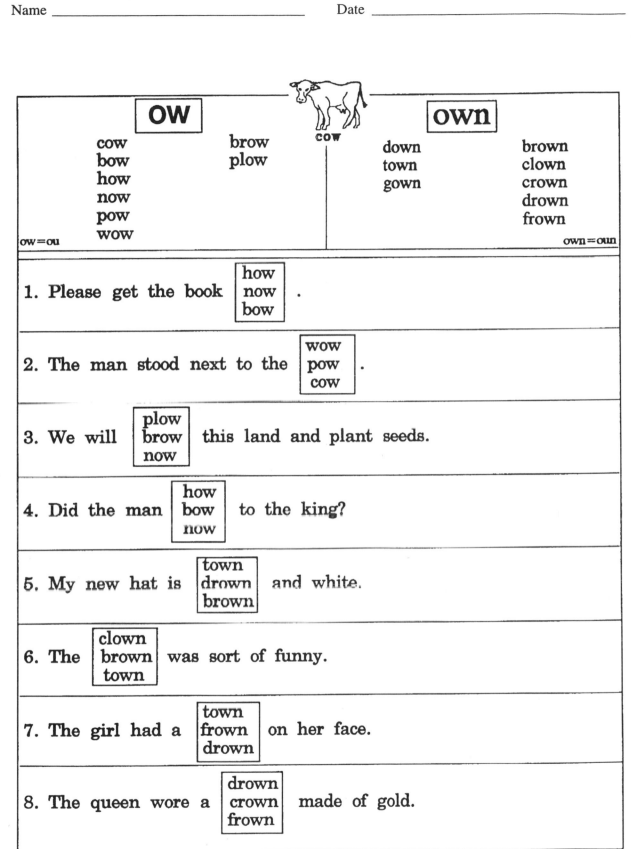

ow		**own**	
cow	brow	down	brown
bow	plow	town	clown
how		gown	crown
now			drown
pow			frown
wow			

ow = ou   own = oun

cow

1. Please get the book ☐ how / now / bow .

2. The man stood next to the ☐ wow / pow / cow .

3. We will ☐ plow / brow / now this land and plant seeds.

4. Did the man ☐ how / bow / now to the king?

5. My new hat is ☐ town / drown / brown and white.

6. The ☐ clown / brown / town was sort of funny.

7. The girl had a ☐ town / frown / drown on her face.

8. The queen wore a ☐ drown / crown / frown made of gold.

Name _____

Date _____

ow

For those who print
1.

stop now

2.

see the cow

For those who use cursive.
1.

stop now

2.

see the cow

Name _____   Date _____

cowboy

Each of the unfinished words below contains the <u>ow</u> sound as in *cow*.
The pupil reads the sentence and writes the missing letters to complete the word.

1. We must _____ ow the farm before it rains.   p   pl   br

2. The _____ ow ate a lot of hay.   n   h   c

3. Mom will let us go to the mall _____ ow.   n   s   b

4. The man would not ___ ow to the king.   h   b   s

5. The ___ own did a lot of funny tricks.   cl   dr   cr

6. Dan will ride his horse into ___own today.   g   d   t

7. My new jacket is ___ own and white.   dr   tr   br

8. The king would not give up his ___own.   dr   cr   br

9. The man was very upset.
   He had a _____ own on his face.   dr   fr   t

10. Help us get the cat out of the well.
    It will _____ own if we don't get it.   dr   cr   cl

211

CHECK LIST

ow

ow = ou

bow	drown	town
brow	frown	wow
brown	gown	
cow	how	
clown	now	
crown	pow	
down	plow	

Additional words that have this ow *sound:*

crowd	power
drowsy	powder
flower	prowler
fowl	shower
growl	towel
howl	tower
owl	trowel

ou

ou = ou

blouse	hour	proud
bound	house	round
bout	loud	scour
couch	louse	scout
cloud	mouse	shout
flour	mouth	slouch
found	out	sound
grouch	pouch	sour
ground	pound	south
hound	pout	spout

Additional words that have this ou *sound:*

bough	flour
bounce	fountain
boundary	mount
bounty	mountain
cloudy	mouth
count	noun
county	thousand
doubt	

I.

oil	**oin**	**oint**
boil broil coil spoil foil soil	coin join	joint point
oil=oil	oin=oin	oint=oint

1. We will _____ this corn for a short time.	soil boil foil
2. Did you _____ the new club at school?	coin join
3. _____ to the place on the map where you are going.	Point Joint
4. This meat will _____ if it isn't kept cool.	coil foil spoil
5. We can put _____ around the meat. It will keep the meat cool.	foil boil coil
6. The _____ was made of pure gold.	coin join

II. _____

Say to the student, "Now that you know how the letters **oi** sound, see if you can figure out what the underlined words are."

1. We could not make out what the speaker was saying.

   The <u>noise</u> was very loud.

2. The food is nice and <u>moist.</u>

Name _____

Date _____

oil

For those who print

1. we will broil

2. it will spoil

For those who use cursive.

1. *we will broil*

2. *it will spoil*

214

Each underlined word has the *oi* sound as in *oil*. Together with the context clues, the student should try to decode the underlined word and read the complete sentence.

1. Who is your <u>choice</u> for leader of the team?   choice

2. This cake is so good and <u>moist</u>.   moist

3. The class was very <u>noisy</u> today.   noisy

4. The <u>oilcan</u> is on the shelf.   oilcan

5. Did the <u>poison</u> kill the bugs?   poison

For 2 players. Use a spinning wheel that has numerals 1-6 on it. The pupil advances the number of spaces if he/she says the words correctly.

claw	spoil	food	spoil	flew	glue	S T O P

paw

suit	book	could	brown	mouse	cow

broil

coin	haul	boil	law	tall	talk	jaw

all

caught	fought	loop	oil	June	fruit

now

G O	wood	town	house	join	point	hope

I.

oy

boy
joy
Roy
toy

boy

oy=oi

1. The name of the little boy is | toy / Roy / joy | .

2. Roy got a new | coy / toy / coy | for his first birthday.

3. The little | joy / coy / boy | took his new toy to school.

4. The storm was over.

   There was a lot of | joy / Roy / toy | in the town.

II. The student reads the first part of the sentence and decides how it should be finished. If he/she can't write the words, the instructor should print them. When all the sentences have been completed the student rereads the completed sentences.

1. My new toy is _____ .

2. The boy gave his _____ .

3. Roy is the name of _____ .

4. Did you enjoy _____ ?

Name _____

Date _____

oy

For those who print

1.

2.

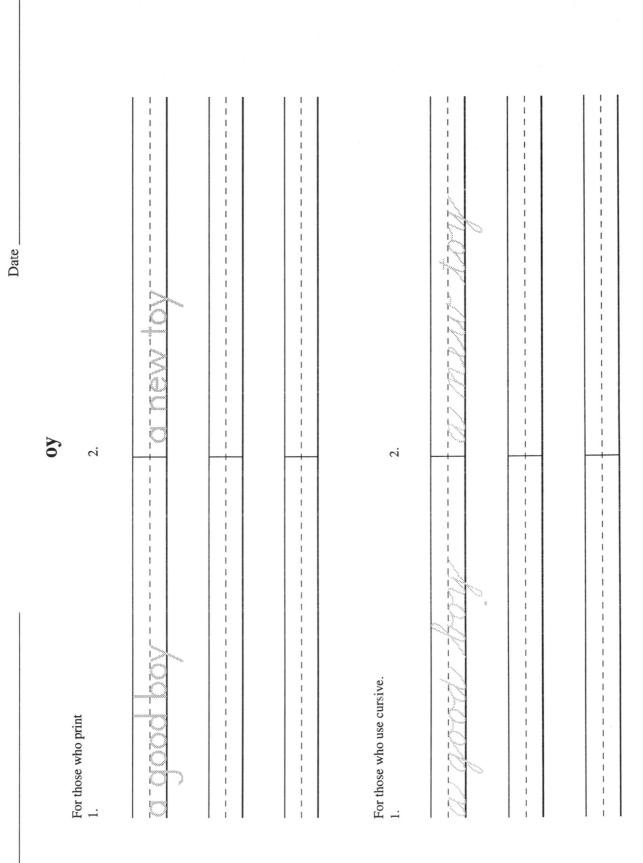

For those who use cursive.

1.

2.

I.   ACROSS   DOWN

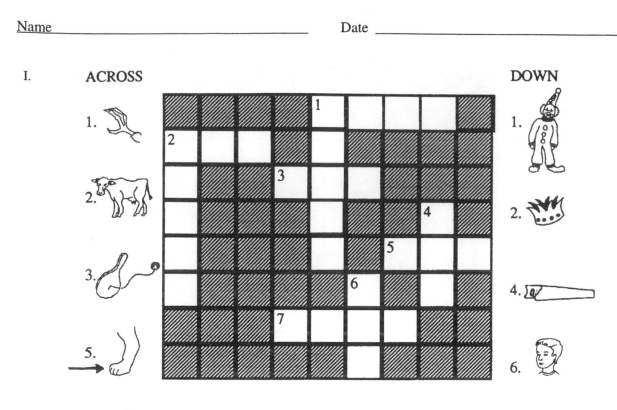

1.

2.

3.

5.

7.

II. Write a rhyming word for each word below:

boy	cow	wall	crown
_____	_____	_____	_____
paw	cook	talk	stew
_____	_____	_____	_____

CHECK LIST

oi

oi = oi

boil	moist
broil	noise
coin	point
coil	poise
foil	soil
hoist	spoil
join	toil
joint	

Additional words that have this oi *sound:*

choice
foist...........to pass off as the real thing
loiter..........to linger idly
noisy
poison
oilcan
ointment
turquoise......greenish-blue semi-precious stone

oy

oy = oi

boy

coy

joy

Roy

toy

Additional words that have this oy *sound:*

loyal
oyster
royal
soybean
toybox
voyage

R–CONTROLLED VOWELS

är

ûr

ôr

ărr

ĕrr

îr ûr är âr

Name _____ Date _____

star ★

ark	ar	art
ark spark bark dark mark park	car star bar far jar tar	art chart cart start dart part tart
ark=ärk	ar=är	art=ärt

1. My dog will not [dark / mark / bark] at you if you stand still.

2. Tom had a good [part / dart / art] in the school play.

3. Mark drew a [tar / star / far] on the book.

4. Hand me the [chart / start], please.

5. When we lit the fire cracker we saw a [dark / park / spark].

6. Dad put [far / tar / bar] on our driveway.

7. Put the food in the [cart / art / dart].

8. A [dark / bark / lark] is a small .

223

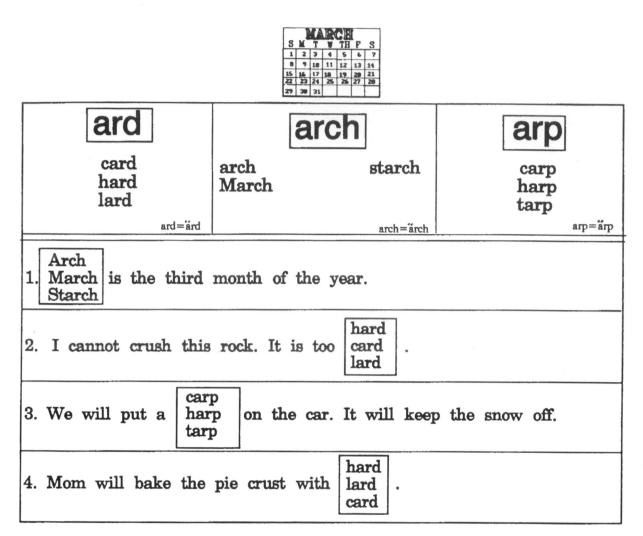

ard	arch	arp
card hard lard	arch starch March	carp harp tarp
ard = ärd	arch = ärch	arp = ärp

1. | Arch / March / Starch | is the third month of the year.

2. I cannot crush this rock. It is too | hard / card / lard | .

3. We will put a | carp / harp / tarp | on the car. It will keep the snow off.

4. Mom will bake the pie crust with | hard / lard / card | .

Each underlined word has the ar sound.
Together with the context clues, the student should be able to figure out the word.

1. The <u>car</u>penter made a house out of wood.   carpenter

2. Would you like to play a game of <u>mar</u>bles?   marbles

3. Do you grow beets in your ga<u>rd</u>en?   garden

4. We had a good time at the <u>par</u>ty.   party

Name _____

Date _____

ark

For those who print

1.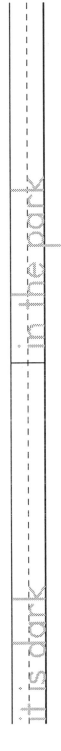

2. in the park

For those who use cursive.

1.

2. *in the park*

225

1. Explain to the pupil that all the pictures in the exercise below begin with the same sound as the word **arm**.
2. Read the following definitions to the pupil as you point to the picture:
   a. The arctic is the extremely cold region that lies north of the Arctic Circle.
   b. Argentina is a country in South America that is located between the South Pacific Ocean and the South Atlantic Ocean.
   c. An archway is an arch covering a passageway.
3. Next, the pupil names the picture and writes the name from the list.

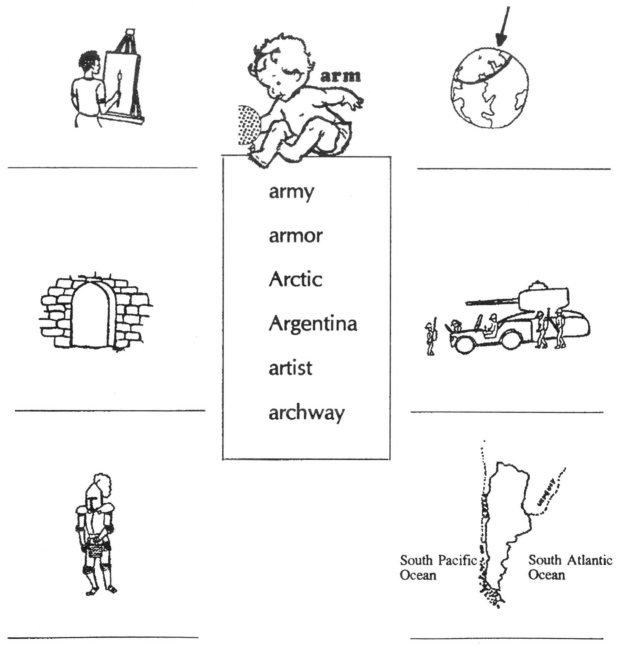

army

armor

Arctic

Argentina

artist

archway

South Pacific Ocean   South Atlantic Ocean

H I D E   'N   S E E K

Draw a line around the hidden picture and write the number on it.

1. car	4. jar	7. cart
2. dart	5. harp	8. card
3. star	6. lark	

CHECK LIST

ar

ar=är

ark	dart	part
arch	far	sharp
bar	hard	spark
bark	harp	star
car	jar	starch
card	lard	start
carp	lark	tar
cart	mark	tarp
chart	March	tart
dark	park	

Additional words that have this **ar** *sound :*

alarm	article	Mars
arbor	artist	marvel
arch	barnyard	marvelous
archway	carpenter	partner
arctic	carve	party
Argentina	farm	sardine
argue	garden	scarf
argument	harbor	sparkle
armor	harm	varnish
army	large	varsity
arsenal	marble	
Arthur	market	

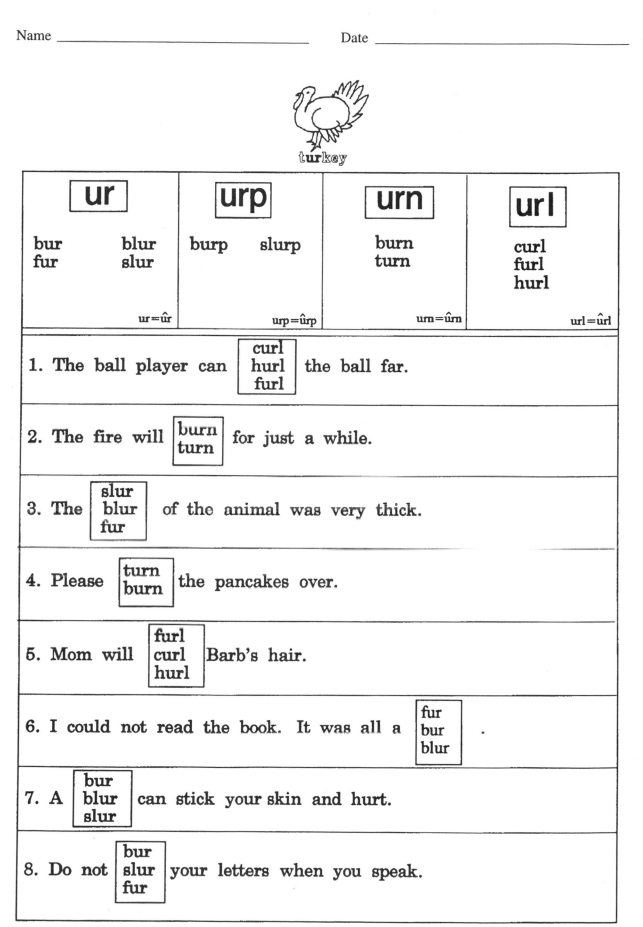

turkey

ur	**urp**	**urn**	**url**
bur blur fur slur	burp slurp	burn turn	curl furl hurl
ur=ûr	urp=ûrp	urn=ûrn	url=ûrl

1. The ball player can [curl / hurl / furl] the ball far.

2. The fire will [burn / turn] for just a while.

3. The [slur / blur / fur] of the animal was very thick.

4. Please [turn / burn] the pancakes over.

5. Mom will [furl / curl / hurl] Barb's hair.

6. I could not read the book. It was all a [fur / bur / blur].

7. A [bur / blur / slur] can stick your skin and hurt.

8. Do not [bur / slur / fur] your letters when you speak.

Name _____

Date _____

urn

For those who print

1. I will burn

2. we can turn

For those who use cursive.

1. I will burn we can turn

2.

Each underlined word has the <u>ur</u> sound as in <u>turtle</u>.
Together with the context clues, the student should try to decode the underlined word and read the complete sentence.

turtle

1. The <u>turtle</u> is a very slow animal.   turtle

2. We had a <u>turkey</u> sandwich for lunch.   turkey

3. <u>Purple</u> is a mix of red and blue.   purple

4. Mom bought a new <u>curtain</u> for the window.   curtain

5. Mom bought new <u>furniture</u> for my bedroom.   furniture

For 2 players. Use a spinning wheel that has numerals 1-6 on it. The pupil advances the number of spaces if he/she says the words correctly.

herb	blur	sir	dirt	chalk	raw	STOP
her						
blue	slaw	shirt	perk	small	turn	bur
						fur
stir	hall	hurl	clerk	draw	crawl	fir
all						
curl	verb	skirt	burn	jerk	twirl	girl
						saw
GO	germ	term	slur	taught	March	soon

231

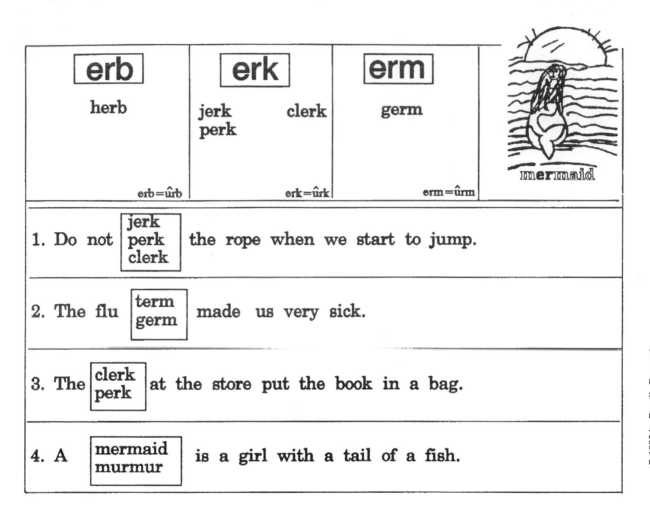

erb	erk	erm	
herb	jerk clerk perk	germ	
erb = ûrb	erk = ûrk	erm = ûrm	mermaid

1. Do not | jerk
perk
clerk | the rope when we start to jump.

2. The flu | term
germ | made us very sick.

3. The | clerk
perk | at the store put the book in a bag.

4. A | mermaid
murmur | is a girl with a tail of a fish.

Each underlined word has the **er** sound as in **mermaid.**
Together with the context clues, the student should try to decode the underlined word and read the complete sentence.

1. The U.S. team had a **perfect** score.   perfect

2. A **termite** is a bug that likes to eat wood.   termite

3. It was 32° on the **thermometer.**   thermometer

4. Did you ever eat strawberry **sherbet?**   sherbet

Name _____

Date _____

erk

For those who print
1.

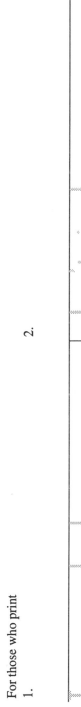

2.

For those who use cursive.
1.

2.

I.

DEFINITIONS

1. Something that can make us sick   _____ herd

2. Someone who helps us in a store   _____ herb

3. Something we can grow in a garden   _____ clerk

4. A sharp twist   _____ germ

5. A lot of animals   _____ jerk

II.

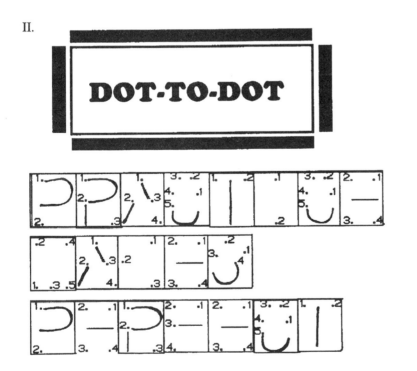

DOT-TO-DOT

_____ _____ _____ _____

Name _____   Date _____

I.

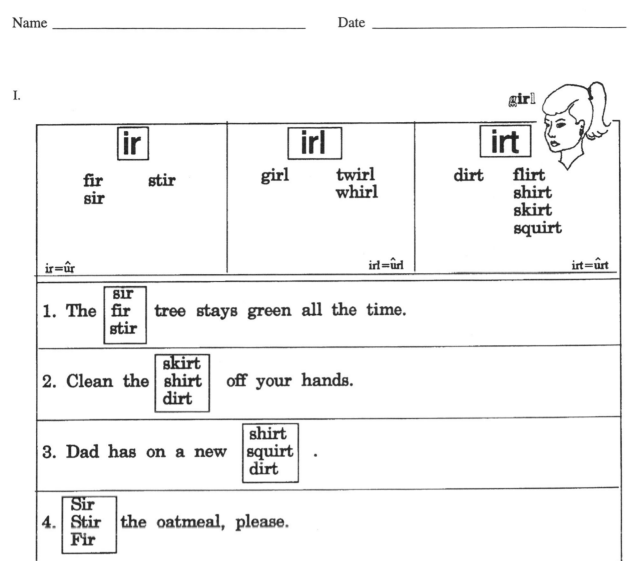

ir	**irl**	**irt**
fir stir sir	girl twirl whirl	dirt flirt shirt skirt squirt
ir = ûr	irl = ûrl	irt = ûrt

1. The | sir
fir
stir | tree stays green all the time.

2. Clean the | skirt
shirt
dirt | off your hands.

3. Dad has on a new | shirt
squirt
dirt | .

4. | Sir
Stir
Fir | the oatmeal, please.

II. The student reads the first part of the sentence and decides how it should be finished. If he/she can't write the words, then the instructor should print it out. When all the sentences have been completed the student rereads them.

1. Did you see the girl twirl the _____ ?

2. "Yes, sir," said the little boy to _____ .

3. The squirt gun _____ .

4. Her new skirt _____ .

235

Name _____

Date _____

ir

For those who print

1. yes sir

2. let me stir

For those who use cursive.

1.

2.

Name _____   Date _____

I.

UNSCRAMBLERS

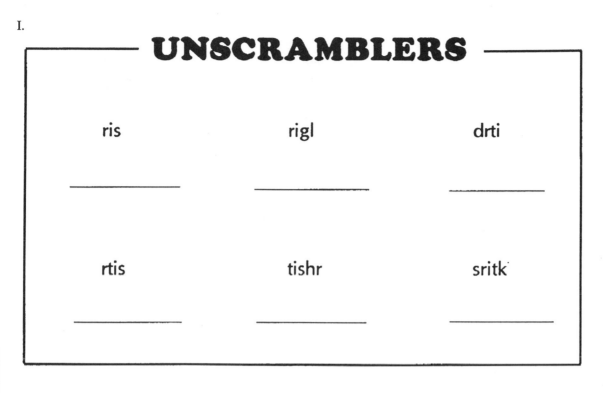

ris   rigl   drti

_____   _____   _____

rtis   tishr   srtik

_____   _____   _____

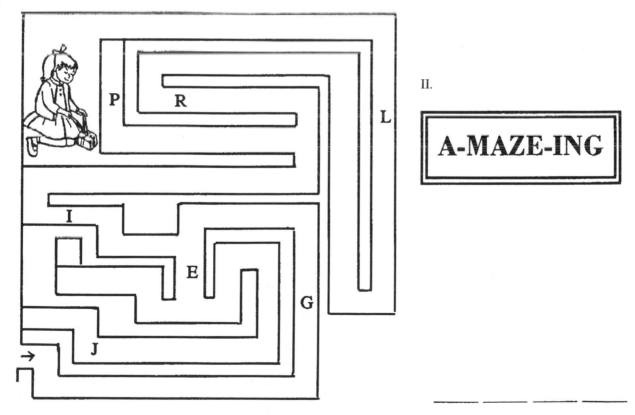

II.

A-MAZE-ING

_____ _____ _____ _____ _____

I.

wor	world
word worm work world worth	

wor = wûr

1. How much is that old car _____ ?

word
world
worth

2. Do you _____ at the mall?

work
word
worth

3. We call our _____ EARTH.

word
world
work

4. Larry put a _____ on the hook for bait.

worth
worm
work

5. Jerry could read every _____ in the book.

work
world
word

II. On the blank line, put the number of the word on the left that matches the definition.

1. workbench _____ someone who works very hard

2. workbag _____ something in which a pupil does homework

3. workbook _____ a place where work is done

4. workhorse _____ a table at which a person works

5. workroom _____ something that holds things a person works with

wor

For those who print

1. they work

2. it's a worm

For those who use cursive.

1. *they work*

2. *it's a worm*

Name _____ Date _____

I.

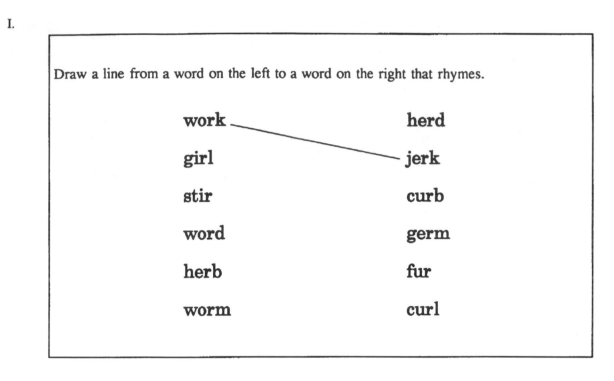

Draw a line from a word on the left to a word on the right that rhymes.

work	herd
girl	jerk
stir	curb
word	germ
herb	fur
worm	curl

II.

Draw a line around all the words on the right that have the same vowel sound as the word on the left.

work	(her)	cart	(stir)	(fur)
perk	worm	girl	turn	here
word	for	curb	dirt	herb
shirt	germ	fir	curl	world
worth	surf	third	store	clerk
burn	bark	verb	firm	work

CHECK LIST

ir

ir=ûr

dirt	shirt
fir	skirt
girl	squirt
sir	twirl
stir	whirl

Additional words that have this ir *sound:*

birch	chirp	giraffe
bird	circus	third
birdbath	dirty	thirsty
birdhouse	firm	thirty
birthday	first	

er

er= ûr

germ	perk
her	term
herb	verb
jerk	

Additional words that have this er *sound:*

certain	mercy	personality
expert	merchant	servant
fern	per cent	sherbet
geranium	perch	thermometer
herd	perfect	thermostat
hermit	performance	
kernel	perhaps	

ur

ur=ûr

bur	curl	slur
burn	fur	slurp
burp	furl	turn
blur	hurl	

Additional words that have this ur *sound :*

burden	disturb	nurse	turnip
burglar	furnace	purchase	turnpike
church	furniture	purple	turtle
churn	hurricane	purpose	
curb	hurry	purse	
curtain	jury	Saturday	
curve	murmur	turkey	

wor

wor=wûr

word	world
worm	worth
work	

Additional words that have this wor *sound :*

word-for-word	world-wide	worship
workbench	wormwood	worst
workbook	worry	worthy

I.

orn	1. This coat is old and [worn / corn / horn] .
born corn horn torn worn	2. We grew this [born / corn / born] in our garden.
orn = ôrn	3. Don't toot the [worn / torn / horn] or you will wake the baby.

corn

II.

ort	1. Mike and Tom will make a [sort / fort / short] to play in.
fort short port sport sort	2. The [port / sort / sport] I like best is football.
ort = ôrt	3. Pat is tall and Pam is [short / sport / port] .

III.

orm	1. We had a snow [storm / form / dorm] here this morning.
form storm dorm	2. Mom will fill out this [dorm / form / storm] and I will take it to school.
orm = ôrm	

IV.

ork	1. You should place the [stork / fork] on the left of the plate.
cork stork fork pork	2. The [pork / stork / cork] is a bird with a long bill and long legs.
ork = ôrk	

Name _____

Date _____

orn

For those who print

1. It is torn

2. Is it worn

For those who use cursive.

1. *It is torn*

2. *Is it worn*

Name _____   Date _____

Each underlined word has the __or__ sound as in *orchestra*.
Together with the context clues, the student should try to decode the underlined word and read the complete sentence.

1. Ned will play his horn in the school <u>orchestra</u>.   orchestra

2. An <u>orange</u> has a lot of good juice.   orange

3. The <u>tornado</u> hit our town and tore down our homes.   tornado

4. Please put the books back in the right <u>order</u>.   order

5. I will tell you a <u>story</u> if you sit still.   story

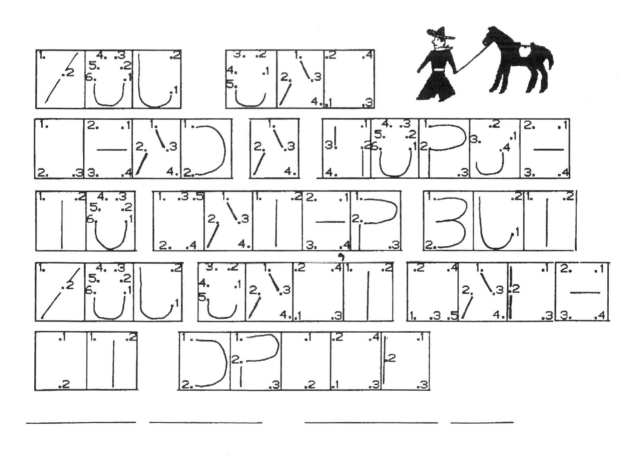

_____ _____ _____ _____

_____ _____ _____ _____

_____ _____ _____ _____

244

Name _____   Date _____

H I D E 'N S E E K

The following objects are hidden in the picture above:
Draw a line around the picture and write the number on it.

1. horn
2. north
3. forty

4. corn
5. stork
6. torpedo

7. fork
8. horse
9. orange

war	

wart hog

war
warn
warp
wart
warm

war = wôr

Before starting this exercise read the following definitions:
   to warp means to bend an object out of shape
   a wart hog is a wild hog that has wartlike growths on each side of its face and has tusks

1. This is a _____ coat.	warm warp wart
2. That hot pan will _____ if you cool it too soon.	war warn warp
3. Did Jerry _____ the crowd about the ice storm?	wart warn warp
4. The men came home from the _____ .	warm warn war
5. The _____ hog has big warts on its face.	wart warn warp
6. The _____ of the fire made us feel better.	wart warmth warp

Name _____

Date _____

war

For those who print

1.

we are warm

2.

it will warp

For those who use cursive.

1.

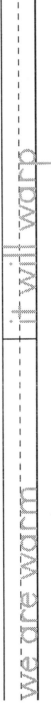

2.

a b c d e f g h i j k l m n o p q r s t u v w x y z

I. Put the words that are in the box in alphabetical order.

warp	ward	warn	wart	warm

1. _____

2. _____

3. _____

4. _____

5. _____

II.

The student reads the first part of the sentence and decides how it should be finished. If he/she can't write it, then the instructor should print it out. When all the sentences have been completed the student rereads them.

1. The war _____ .

2. We will warn _____ .

3. The _____ is nice and warm.

4. The _____ had war paint on his face.

5. The wart on his hand _____ .

CHECK LIST

or

		or = ôr

born	porch
corn	scorch
cork	short
dorm	sport
fort	storm
fork	stork
horn	torn
port	torch
pork	worn

Additional words that have this or *sound :*

border	morning	orbit	orient
cord	New York	orchard	orphan
corner	normal	orchestra	port
for	north	order	story
forty	Norway	organ	tornado
horse	orange	organization	torpedo

war

	war = wŏr

war

warm

warmth

Additional words that have the ar *sound:*

warble...........to sing as birds sing
warden..........the head of a prison
warranty........a promise backing up a claim
Warsaw........ a city in the country of Poland

warn

warp

Name _____ Date _____

I.

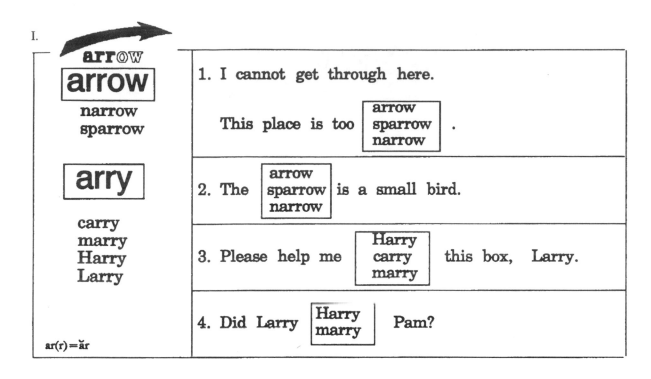

arrow

arrow

narrow
sparrow

arry

carry
marry
Harry
Larry

ar(r) = ăr

1. I cannot get through here.

   This place is too | arrow / sparrow / narrow | .

2. The | arrow / sparrow / narrow | is a small bird.

3. Please help me | Harry / carry / marry | this box, Larry.

4. Did Larry | Harry / marry | Pam?

II.

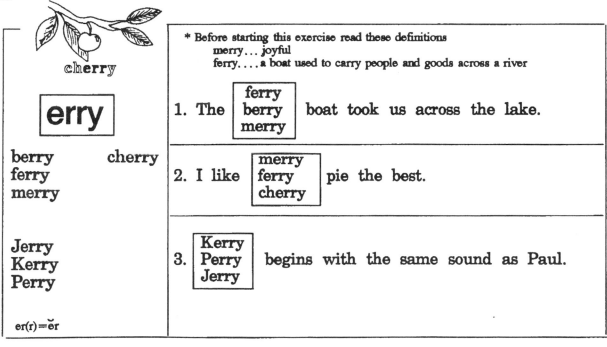

cherry

erry

berry   cherry
ferry
merry

Jerry
Kerry
Perry

er(r) = ĕr

* Before starting this exercise read these definitions
    merry... joyful
    ferry.... a boat used to carry people and goods across a river

1. The | ferry / berry / merry | boat took us across the lake.

2. I like | merry / ferry / cherry | pie the best.

3. | Kerry / Perry / Jerry | begins with the same sound as Paul.

250

Name _____ Date _____

err

For those who print

1. she is Larry   he is Jerry

2.

For those who use cursive.

1.

2.

Name _____   Date _____

I. Things That Go Together

pie   Christmas   boat   nest   arrow

1. bow and _____

2. sparrow and _____

3. Merry _____

4. cherry _____

5. ferry _____

II.

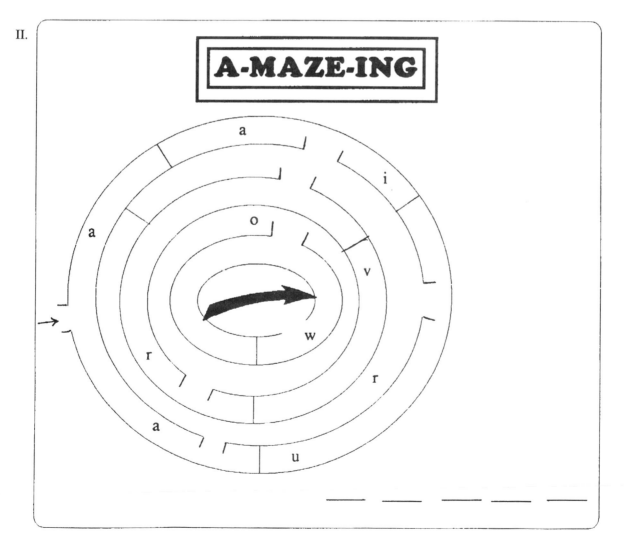

A-MAZE-ING

a i o v w r r a u

_____ _____ _____ _____ _____ _____

CHECK LIST

ar(r)

ar(r)=ăr

arrow

carry

Harry

Additional Words that have this ar(r) *sound:*

Larry

barracks........military living quarters
barracuda.......a large, savage fish from the waters north of Brazil
barrel

marry

barricade........barrier made in a hurry for protection
barrier...........something that bars entrance
carriage

narrow

carrot
marriage

sparrow

parrot

er(r)

er(r)=ĕr

berry

cherry

ferry

Additional words that have this er(r) *sound:*

merry

blueberry
cranberry
derrick
errand

Jerry

error
ferris wheel

Kerry

herring..............small fish that can be prepared for eating
terrible
terrify

Perry

territory
terry cloth

FOUR SOUNDS FOR **ear**

1. ear (îr) as in spear

2. ear (ûr) as in pearl

3. ear (är) as in heart

4. ear (âr) as in bear

I.

spear

dear   spear
fear   clear
hear
near
tear
year

ear = îr

1. Did you _____ the sound of the bell?	dear hear year
2. The sound of the bell was _____ .	year spear clear
3. Next _____ our class will go to New York.	year tear fear
4. Ann sat _____ Andy.	hear near tear

II.

pearl

pearl
Earl

earn
learn

ear = ûr

1. Mom bought Sue a _____ pin.	Earl pearl
2. I will _____ to play a brass horn.	earn learn
3. _____ is the name of the boy.	Pearl Earl
4. I can _____ a coin for helping Dad.	learn earn

Name _____ Date _____

(four Sounds for **ear** continued)

III.

heart

heart
hearty
hearth

ear=är

1. Did your _____ pound when you won?	heart hearty
2. The _____ of the fireplace is brick.	hearty hearth
3. We had some _____ soup for lunch.	hearth hearty

IV.

bear

bear
pear
tear

ear-âr

1. A _____ is good for a snack.	tear pear bear
2. The box will _____ if you drop it.	tear bear
3. The _____ has thick fur and a short tail.	pear tear bear

ear

For those who print

1. can you hear

2. it is clear

For those who use cursive.

1. can you hear

2. it is clear

Name _____

Date _____

ear

For those who print

1.

earn it

2.

learn it

For those who use cursive.

1.

2.

Name _____

Date _____

ear

For those who print

1. big heart

2. stone hearth

For those who use cursive.

1. *big heart*

2. *stone hearth*

258

Name _____

Date _____

ear

For those who print

1.

2.

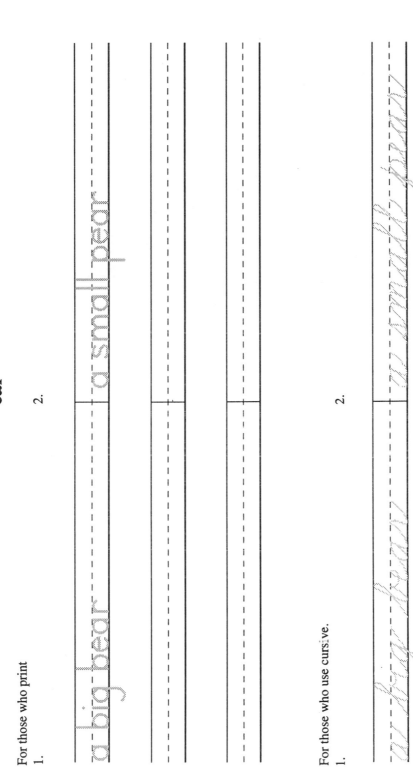

a big bear

a small pear

For those who use cursive.

1.

2.

259

H I D E 'N S E E K

The following objects are hidden in the picture above.
Draw a line around the picture and write the number on it.

1. head
2. feather
3. steak

4. bread
5. peach
6. spear

7. thread
8. pearl
9. heart

CHECK LIST

ear
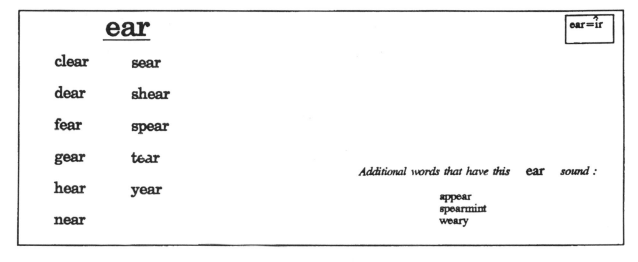

		ear=îr

clear	sear
dear	shear
fear	spear
gear	tear
hear	year
near	

Additional words that have this **ear** *sound :*

appear
spearmint
weary

ear

ear=âr

bear

pear

tear

ear

ear=ûr

Earl

earn

learn

pearl

Additional words that have this **ear** *sound :*

early	heard	search
earth	hearse	

ear

ear=är

heart

hearth

hearty

Additional word that has this **ear** *sound:*

hearken.....to listen carefully

Answer Keys

PART ONE

Page 3 (short *a*)

    1. cat   5. sad

    2. rat   6. rat

    3. Dad   7. Pat

    4. bat

Page 5 (short *a*)

I.

cat,   hat

sad,   mad

mat,   bat

glad,   rat

II. B, A, A, B

Page 7 (short *a*)

    1. tag   4. jam

    2. flag   5. swam

    3. rag   6. Pam

Page 9 (short *a*)

  I. B, D, A, C

II.

tag,   bag

rag,   wag

ham,   dam

jam,   clam

Page 10 (short a̱)

FLAG

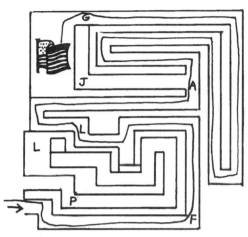

Page 11 (short a̱)

fan, Dan, map, clap, plan

Page 13 (short a)

I.

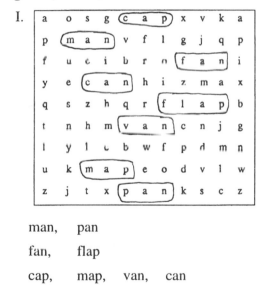

man,   pan

fan,   flap

cap,   map,   van,   can

II. fat, tag, cap, pan, ham, sad

Page 14 (short a̱)

fan, man, tap, clap, trap

Page 15 (short a̱)

I. jam, rag, bag, man

cap, fan, ham, can

cat, bad, hat, flag

Pam, sad, clap, slam

II. van, map, Dad, the, had, a, in

Dad had a map in the van.

Page 16 (short _a_)

1. dash   5. track
2. rash   6. cash
3. pack   7. snack
4. crash

Page 18 (short _a_)

I.

a	t	h	e	u	k	b	f	p	a
s	m	t	r	a	c	k	b	o	l
v	a	n	x	i	d	c	o	y	j
o	n	e	u	t	c	a	s	h	p
k	g	w	b	l	a	c	k	z	d
w	q	t	a	c	k	x	c	n	i
a	o	v	l	q	r	s	f	u	e
d	e	r	v	b	s	h	a	c	k
c	r	a	s	h	g	m	h	i	y
z	f	j	g	c	b	a	t	b	z

tack, cash

shack, crash

black, track

van, bat

II. Rhyming words will vary.

Page 20 (short _a_)

ambulance, ax

ant, alligator

antelope, alphabet

address, add

Page 22 (long _a_)

1. gave   5. lame
2. tame   6. Save
3. game   7. same
4. cave

Page 24 (long _a_)

I.

tape,	game
cave,	wave
tack,	sack
cash,	wag

II.
1. sāme	6. cāve	11. lăp
2. băck	7. cāme	12. wăve
3. gāme	8. năg	13. glăd
4. căsh	9. sāve	14. hăm
5. gāve	10. căt	15. tāme

Page 25 (long _a_)

I. game, tame, cave

II.
Across	Down
1. game	1. gas
3. sad	2. wag
5. bag	4. dad
7. ham	6. cave
9. vet	8. map
11. cap	10. tag
12. ten	11. cat

Page 26 (long _a_)

1. mail	6. lay
2. rain	7. nail
3. hay	8. pain
4. pail	9. sail
5. train	

Page 28 long _a_)

I.

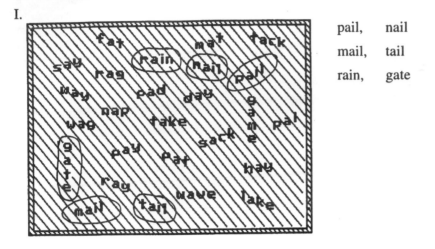

pail,   nail
mail,   tail
rain,   gate

II. payday, mailman, hatrack, backpack, nametag, cattail

Page 29 (long _a_)

I. pāin, măd, pāy, tāme, băt

hāy, rāin, cāne, sāve, gāve

dāy, pāve, māy, tăg

căp, pāid, flăp, flăg, crăck

cāve, păck, glăd, căsh, făn

BINGO: second row from the top

II. pail, tag, mail, bat, pain

Page 30 (long _a_)

1. pace   4. fake
2. rake   5. lace
3. face   6. cake

Page 32 (long _a_)

I.   A. 2;   B. 1;   C. 1;   D. 2;   E. 2

II.   CAKE

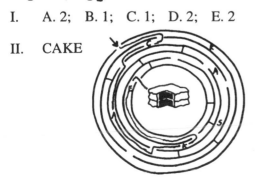

Page 34 (short *e*)

1. pen   5. stem
2. hem   6. Ten
3. men   7. hen
4. den

Page 36 (short *e*)

II. *Across*   *Down*

1. hen   1. hem
2. men   3. ten
4. leg   5. gem
6. pen

II. old man; a black pen

a hen; beg

bat; ham

Page 37 (short *e*)

hen, tag

rat, cake

stem, pen

men, cap

Page 38 (short *e*)

1. fell   5. vest
2. nest   6. pest
3. rest   7. shell
4. Tell

Page 40 (short *e*)

I.

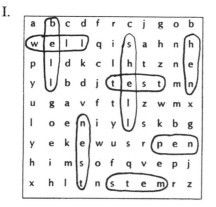

bell, well

hen, pen

test, nest

shell, stem

II. shell, vest

bell, pail

cap, beg

net, pest

Page 41 (short _e_)

I. 1. nest   6. fell

2. test   7. sell

3. vest   8. yell

4. rest   9. well

5. best

II. bell, mat, vest

flag, map, men

Rhyming words will vary.

Page 42 (short _e_)

1. fed   3. Ted

2. pet   4. wet

Page 44 (short _e_)

II. _Across_   _Down_

1. bed   1. bell

2. sled   3. jet

4. ten   5. net

6. vet

II. ham, cash, Dad

May, pain, race

bed, test, jet

Page 46 (short _e_)

1. leg   5. deck

2. beg   6. peck

3. eggs   7. check

4. check

Page 48 (short _e_)

II. *Across*   *Down*

   3. ape   1. leg

   4. game   2. jam

   6. check   5. chest

   7. sack

II. cake, nest

   pen, face

   bell, leg

   map, bat

   sack, neck

Page 49 (short _e_)

neck, check, vest, vet, bell

Page 50 (short _e_)

elk, empty

excavator, elf

envelope

egg, Eskimo

Page 52 (long _e_)

   1. feed   4. feet

   2. meet   5. seed

   3. weed

Page 54 (long _e_)

I. 1, 1, 2, 1, 1

II. TREE

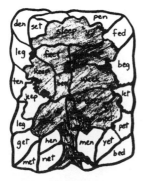

Page 55 (long e̱)

   1. meet   4. feed
   2. deed   5. weed
   3. seed   6. sheet

Page 56 (long e̱)

   1. week   5. check
   2. deep   6. sheep
   3. peek   7. sleep
   4. keep

Page 58 (long e̱)

   1. chick   5. jcep
   2. calendar   6. boy
   3. car   7. sheep
   4. lake

Page 59 (long e̱)

I.   chēek, wēed, tĕst, jēep, dĕck
     fēet, bĕll, nĕt, sēed, bĕt
     nēed, nĕck, crēep, pĕst
     slēep, fēed, dēep, bēet, pēek
     thĕn, sēek, wĕb, lĕt, ĕnd
     BINGO: the fourth row from the top

II. weed, jeep
     feet, seed
     beet, sheep
     tree, bee

Page 60 (long e̱)

   1. team   5. mean
   2. beat   6. wheat
   3. lean   7. weak
   4. leak

Page 62 (long *e*)

I. 1. team   4. heat

  2. seat   5. meat

  3. team

II. TEAM

Page 63 (long *e*)

I.   meat, stem

    lake, rain

    wheat, seat

    men, check

II.   Easter, easel

    eel, East

Page 64 (long *e*)

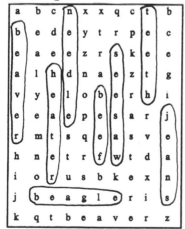

beef   jeans

teeth   heater

needle   beaver

seesaw   beagle

Page 66 (short *i*)

I. 1. Sit   4. rid

  2. hid   5. lid

  3. bit

II. 1. bat (S)   4. west (S)   7. itch (S)   10. race (L)

2. sail (L)   5. lid (S)   8. cheap (L)   11. bit (S)

3. mitt (S)   6. seed (L)   9. cash (S)   12. peep (L)

Page 68 (short _i_)

I. Rhyming words will vary.

II. ALL THAT GLITTERS IS NOT GOLD

Page 70 (short _i_)

1. dig   5. chin

2. fin   6. pig

3. wig   7. thin

4. pin

Page 72 (short _i_)

I. pig, bat

big, lid

pin, hat

fan, pet

rag, mitt

II.

```
a  m  f  i  n  l  h  u  a
i  b  g  j  c  h  i  n  e      pin, fin
u  p  i  g  k  q  d  q  f      pig, wig
g  c  k  w  m  r  s  x  i      shin, chin
m  r  b  n  w  i  g  n  v
p  i  n  j  c  t  w  p  l
y  o  e  v  d  s  h  i  n
h  x  p  w  f  b  i  g  o
z  u  t  h  i  n  a  y  z
```

Page 73 (short _i_)

1. hatpin   4. jigsaw

2. pigtail   5. shipshape

3. backpack   6. chin-deep

Page 74 (short _i_)

1. fill   5. pick

2. sick   6. chick

3. bill   7. thick

4. mill

Page 76 (short _i_)

1. hill	6. thick
2. pill	7. lick
3. fill	8. chick
4. bill	9. pick
5. Rick	10. wick

Page 78 (short _i_)

1. him	5. sip
2. tip	6. dim
3. Fish	7. hip
4. rim	

Page 80 (short _i_)

1. sip	6. pin	11. tick	16. fit
2. big	7. tip	12. tin	17. pit
3. sick	8. sit	13. did	18. pick
4. lip	9. hid	14. fin	19. flip
5. hit	10. wig	15. him	20. clip

Page 81 (short _i_)

DON'T GIVE UP THE SHIP

Page 82 (short _i_)

Indian, Italy

ill, insect, infant

Page 84 (long _i_)

1. hide	5. wide
2. bike	6. hide
3. dike	7. side
4. hike	

Page 86 (long _i_)

1. bike	4. Jean
2. take a hike	5. Jake
3. when the tide is out	

Page 87 (long _i_)

I. 1. side	3. bike
2. bike	4. slide

II. BIKE

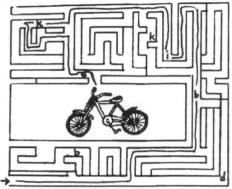

Page 88 (long *i*)

1. high   5. tight
2. lie   6. night
3. sight   7. tie
4. pie

Page 90 (long *i*)

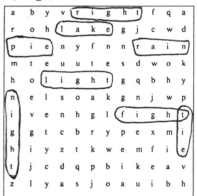

right, fight
pie, tie
night, light
lake, rain

Page 91 (long *i*)

I. 1. hayride   3. hitchhike
   2. tiepin   4. flashlight

II.   *Across*   *Down*
      1. light   1. lip
      3. pin   2. tie
      6. chimp   4. night
                        5. bike
                        6. cat
                        7. pie

Page 92 (long _i_)

1. mile	5. rice
2. ripe	6. file
3. pile	7. pipe
4. Wipe	

Page 94 (long _i_)

I. pipe, file, rice

   mice, ripe, lice

   wipe, mile, nice

II. Sentences will vary.

Page 95 (long _i_)

nīce, bīke, hīde, nīght, sĭck

bĭd, dĭg, tīe, rīpe, dĭsh

rīde, lĭp, hīke, fīght

dĭm, fīle, fĭsh, bĭll, pĭn

līe, rīce, mīle, wīpe, brīght

BINGO: last row of words across bottom

II. 1. pipe	9. mice
2. wave	10. dice
3. pin	11. pie
4. net	12. tie
5. jeep	13. night
6. backpack	14. sheep
7. game	15. rain
8. beak	16. ray

Page 96 (long _i_)

1. dime	5. Five
2. mine	6. chime
3. dive	7. nine
4. time	

Page 98 (long _i_)

   I. 1. bite   6. pine

       2. dime   7. ride

       3. fine   8. ripe

       4. hide   9. shine

       5. kite   10. slime

  II. A CAT HAS NINE LIVES

Page 100 (short _o_)

     1. pot   5. rock

     2. lock   6. sock

     3. cot   7. tot

     4. shock

Page 102 (short _o_)

   I. 1. dock   4. got

       2. hot   5. rock

       3. shock   6. dot

  II. 1. sŏck   6. pĕck   11. māid

       2. măsh   7. lŏck   12. shŏck

       3. tāme   8. mēan   13. dŏt

       4. pŏt   9. tīme   14. rīght

       5. tēam   10. nŏt   15. wĕst

Page 103 (short _o_)

  I. clock, dot, sock, pot, rock

  II. CLOCK

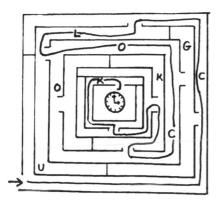

Page 104 (short *o*)

1. hop	5. chop
2. box	6. rod
3. shop	7. mop
4. fox	

Page 106 (short *o*)

Across	*Down*
3. lock	1. rock
4. sock	2. hot
6. box	5. fox
8. mop	7. dot
10. top	9. pot
12. rod	11. cot

Page 107 (short *o*)

A fox on a box

A fish on a rod

A man and a map

An ax that can chop

Page 108 (short *o*)

1. job	4. cog
2. dog	5. sob
3. jog	6. log

Page 110 (short *o*)

bottle, rocket

dominoes, pocket

topping, lobster

locket, popsicle

Page 111 (short *o*)

I. 1. dogfight	4. cogwheel
2. bobcat	5. hilltop
3. eggnog	

II. YOU CAN'T TEACH AN OLD DOG NEW TRICKS

Page 112 (short *o*)

octagon, odd

oxen, otter

Page 114 (long o)

1. hole
2. poke
3. tone
4. pole

5. joke
6. cone
7. woke

Page 115 (long o)

1. home
2. slope
3. rope
4. nose

5. hose
6. hope
7. Rome

Page 117 (long o)

I. joke, more, bone

tore, pole, tone, woke

role, hope, wore, poke

rose, sore, cone, nose

II. CONE

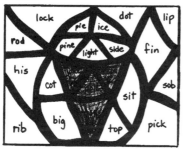

Page 118 (long o)

dome	cone
lone	pole
mole	joke
poke	lone
rope	mole
rode	woke

Page 119 (lone o)

1. road
2. loan
3. boat
4. hoe

5. toad
6. goat
7. toe

Page 121 (long o)

I.

boat, coat

doe, toe

toad, road

soap, hoe

II. 1. feet   6. ice cream

    2. coat   7. face

    3. bone   8. pole

    4. slippers   9. stem

    5. weed   10. hop

Page 122 (long o)

    A. toad   E. hoe

    B. van   F. toe

    C. coat   G. oats

    D. doe

Page 123 (long o)

    1. bow   5. bow

    2. show   6. row

    3. row   7. low

    4. mow

Page 125 (long o)

I. 1. show   5. snow

    2. row   6. row

    3. bow   7. low

    4. mow

II. 1. rowboat   4. slowpoke

    2. snowflake   5. glowworm

    3. blowout

Page 126 (long o)

I.   mōre, rŏck, pōke, bōne, hōle

    shŏp, rōw, tōe, rŏd, cŏb

    cōat, dŏg, fŏx, shōw

clŏck, dŏt, mōw, hōse, fŏg

hōe, bŏx, sōap, frŏg, cŏt

BINGO: the third column from the left

II.   ROW ROW ROW YOUR BOAT

Page 128 (short u̲)

fun, lunch, munch, punch, hunch, bunch, lunch

Page 130 (short u̲)

MAKE HAY WHILE THE SUN SHINES

Page 131 (short u̲)

gum, bump, lump, hum, Pump, jump, thump

Page 133 (short u)

I. 1. lunchtime   3. dumptruck

   2. runway   4. hubcap

II. 1. shĕll   6. hĭll   11. wēep   16. chĕst

   2. sīght   7. lāme   12. tīme   17. māin

   3. căsh   8. hŭmp   13. shŏck   18. pŭnch

   4. lŭnch   9. chēat   14. pīe   19. gŭm

   5. mōw   10. hōle   15. bōw   20. nĕck

Page 134 (short u̲)

I. 1. sum   5. bump

   2. jump   6. gum

   3. dump   7. pump

   4. lump   8. hum

II. 1. gum   4. thump

   2. dump   5. jump

   3. sum   6. bump

Page 135 (short u̲)

cub, duck, buck, hub, sub, puck, tub

Page 137 (short u̲)

I. 1. sāilor   6. tōaster   11. wĭndow   16. răbbit

   2. shŏpper   7. dĕntist   12. tōenail   17. rŭbber

   3. māilman   8. fīghter   13. clēaner   18. sideshow

   4. tēpee   9. ăpple   14. pĭcnic

   5. bŭtter   10. sŭbway   15. cŏpper

Page 138 (short _u_)

I. *Across*

    3. cup

    4. tub

    5. gum

    6. sun

    9. nut

   10. pump

Down

    1. duck

    2. truck

    5. gun

    7. club

    8. bun

II. 1. cab, cob

    2. tab

    3. pack, peck, pick, pock

    4. back

    5. lack, lick, lock

Page 140 (short _u_)

rug, nut, dug, bug, shut, hug, hut

Page 142 (short _u_)

I.

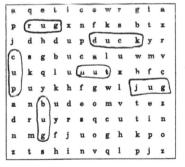

bug, jug

nut, cup

rug, duck

II.   fan, fin, fun

       hat, hit, hot, hut

       ham, hem, him, hum

       rib, rob, rub

       bat, bet, bit, but

       sack, sick, sock, suck

       rag, rig, rug

Page 143 (short _u_)

untied, upper case

under, ugly

Page 147 (long u̲)

  I. 1. cute   3. fuse

     2. cube   4. huge

  II. 1. hūge (L)   6. gŭm (S)   11. bŭnch (S)

     2. dŭck (S)   7. cūte (L)   12. fūel (L)

     3. bŭmp (S)   8. ūse (L)   13. hŭg (S)

     4. cūbe (L)   9. fūse (L)   14. cūe (L)

     5. ŭs (S)   10. cŭt (S)   15. fŭss (S)

Page 149 (long u̲)

  I. mule, cube, fuse, huge

    cute, use, fume, fuel

  II. MULE

Page 150 (long u̲)

  I. dŭck, thŭmp, rŭn, hŭt, mūle

    bŭnch, jŭmp, lŭck, lŭnch, cūte

    fūel, gŭm, dŭmp, fūse

    bŭg, lŭnch, tŭb, bŭmp, hūge

    ūse, dŭg, sŭm, rŭg, cūbe

    BINGO: fifth column from the left

  II. CUBE

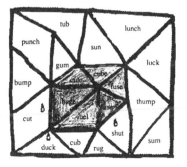

Page 152 (long *u*)

I. 1. cube   5. pupil

  2. huge   6. unicorn

  3. music   7. fuse

  4. uniform   8. unicycle

II. Stories will vary.

PART TWO

Page 159

  1. paw   5. raw

  2. lawn   6. fawn

  3. shawl   7. bawl

  4. slaw   8. Draw

Page 161

saw

paw

claw

hawk

shawl

Page 162

I. 1. Paul   4. pause

  2. maul   5. cause

  3. haul

II. Answers will vary.

Page 164

automat, Australia

August, auger

auk, automobile

Page 165

I. 1. wall   3. mall
    2. call   4. stall

II. 1. talk   3. chalk
    2. walk   4. Stalk

Page 167

I. 1. ballplayer   4. smallpox
    2. fallout   5. wallpaper
    3. hallway

II. walk, chalk, hall
    talk, ball, stalk

Page 168

I. 1. caught
    2. taught
    3. taught

II. 1. brought   5. ought
    2. bought   6. brought
    3. thought   7. fought
    4. fought

Page 172

    1. book   5. brook
    2. hook   6. cook
    3. shook   7. Look
    4. took   8. nook

Page 174

I. 1. full
    2. Pull
    3. bull

II. Answers will vary.

Page 177

1. moon	5. noon
2. tool	6. fool
3. zoo	7. spoon
4. pool	8. moose

Page 179

I. Answers will vary.

II. pool, soup, room

group, fool, noon

Page 181

Page 182

1. flew	5. threw
2. new	6. stew
3. chew	7. drew
4. dew	8. brew

Page 184

I. 1. stew   4. soup

2. threw   5. group

3. dew   6. croup

II. BAD NEWS TRAVELS FAST

Page 185

I. 1. tune

2. June

3. dune

II. 1. glue

2. due

3. blue

III. 1. fruit

2. suit

3. bruise

Page 188

III. new—blue, chew

June—tune, prune

zoo—stew, glue

boot—fruit, root

Page 192

1. bread   5. health

2. weather   6. feather

3. breath   7. read

4. spread   8. thread

Page 196

1. freight   5. reins

2. veins   6. sleigh

3. eight   7. weight

4. weigh

Page 198

   I. B, A, A, B, A, B, B, A

   II. LOVE THY NEIGHBOR AS THYSELF

Page 199

   II. B, A, A, B, A, B

Page 205

1. mouse	5. south
2. found	6. couch
3. spout	7. proud
4. shout	8. sound

Page 208

II. EVERY CLOUD HAS A SILVER LINING

Page 209

1. now	5. brown
2. cow	6. clown
3. plow	7. frown
4. bow	8. crown

Page 211

1. plow	6. town
2. cow	7. brown
3. now	8. crown
4. bow	9. frown
5. clown	10. drown

Page 213

I. 1. boil	4. spoil
2. join	5. foil
3. Point	6. coin

Page 216

    I. 1. Roy   3. boy

        2. toy   4. joy

    II. Answers will vary.

Page 218

    I.   *Across*   *Down*

        1. claw   1. clown

        2. cow   2. crown

        3. toy   4. saw

        5. paw   6. boy

        7. moon

    II. Answers will vary.

Page 223

        1. bark   5. spark

        2. part   6. tar

        3. star   7. cart

        4. chart   8. lark

Page 224

        1. March   3. tarp

        2. hard   4. lard

Page 226

        artist, Arctic

        archway, army

        armor, Argentina

Page 227

Page 229

1. hurl	5. curl
2. burn	6. blur
3. fur	7. bur
4. turn	8. slur

Page 232

1. jerk	3. clerk
2. germ	4. mermaid

Page 234

I.   5, 3, 2, 1, 4

II.   PRACTICE MAKES PERFECT

Page 235

I. 1. fir	3. shirt
2. dirt	4. Stir

II. Answers will vary.

Page 237

  I. sir, girl, dirt

    stir, shirt, skirt

  II. GIRL

Page 238

  I. 1. worth   4. worm

    2. work   5. word

    3. world

  II. 4, 3, 5, 1, 2

Page 240

  I. work—jerk   word—herd

    girl—curl   herb—curb

    stir—fur   worm—germ

  II. work—her, stir, fur

    perk—worm, girl, turn

    word—curb, dirt, herb

    shirt—fir, germ, curl, world

    worth—surf, third, clerk

    burn—firm, verb, work

Page 242

    I. 1. worn

      2. born

      3. horn

   II. 1. fort

      2. sport

      3. short

  III. 1. storm

      2. form

  IV. 1. fork

      2. stork

Page 244

YOU CAN LEAD A HORSE TO WATER BUT YOU CAN'T MAKE IT DRINK

Page 245

Page 246

    1. warm   4. war

    2. warp   5. wart

    3. warn   6. warmth

Page 248

  I. 1. ward   4. warp

    2. warm   5. wart

    3. warn

  II. Answers will vary.

Page 250

  I. 1. narrow   3. carry

    2. sparrow   4. marry

  II. 1. ferry

    2. cherry

    3. Perry

Page 252

  I. 1. arrow   4. pie

    2. nest   5. boat

    3. Christmas

  II. ARROW

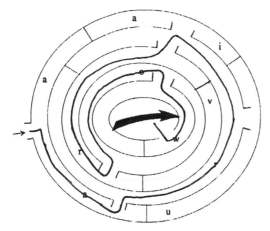

Page 254

    I. 1. hear   3. year

        2. clear   4. near

   II. 1. pearl   3. Earl

       2. learn   4. earn

 III. 1. heart

       2. hearth

       3. hearty

 IV. 1. pear

       2. tear

       3. bear

Page 260